LEGACY *of* LOVE

WHEN HEAVEN HOLDS THE DESTINY OF YOUR CHILD

bndsawyer

To God be all the glory!
—the Connie & Bonnie Sawyer, Jr. Family

Order this book online at www.trafford.com
or email orders@trafford.com

Most Trafford titles are also available at major online book retailers.

Scripture quotations are taken from the King James Version (KJV), New Living
Translation (NLT), New International Version (NIV), and the Message Bible.

Printed in the United States of America.

ISBN: 978-1-4907-3181-0 (sc)
ISBN: 978-1-4907-3183-4 (hc)
ISBN: 978-1-4907-3182-7 (e)

Library of Congress Control Number: 2014905683

Trafford rev. 10/31/2017

www.trafford.com

North America & international
toll-free: 1 888 232 4444 (USA & Canada)
fax: 812 355 4082

CONTENTS

DEDICATION

This work is in memory of my parents, Melvin and Mamie Downing, Sr. In addition, I dedicate this work to my husband's parents, Connie and Shirley Sawyer, Sr. I appreciate them for walking out their faith before us. For their godly examples of a holy lifestyle, I will be forever grateful. I believe that my family is blessed because of the legacy of our parents and their obedience to God.

Melvin and Mamie Downing, Sr.

Connie and Shirley Sawyer, Sr.

ACKNOWLEDGMENTS

T o God be all the glory! I would not have made it without His grace, mercy, and love. In addition, I would like to thank the following persons for helping me with this labor of love. I appreciate your prayers, support, editing, contributions, suggestions, and help with pictures. Connie, Jr. (CC) you have been my strongest supporter and motivator. Thank you for praying for me and helping me to keep the fire of this dream alive. I give special thanks and appreciation to my children and grandchildren: Connie, III, Alicia, Lauryn, Connie, IV, Joshua, Sh'Rhonda, Tiana, Jashon, Janae, Quinton, Lauren, Portia, Leasia, Amaya, Nia, Crystal, Patrick, Kellie, Anthony, Bonney, RJ, Asheton, Carter, and Raymond. Thank you, Naomi, Roderick, Ina, Jennifer, Karen, Val, Gregory Johnson Photography, TEP Studios, Andre Dalton with Aviid Photography, and Don Fields Photography. Also, thanks to RBC Ministries for allowing me to use an excerpt from *Our Daily Bread,* © 2010.

Although I may not have called you by name, you know who you are. Thank you to my Downing Family. Thank you to my Sawyer Family. Thank you to my neighbors and friends. Thank you to my church family. Thank you for all of your help, support, prayers, words of encouragement, gifts, care, and concern down through the years.

PREFACE

I t took spousal prompting to write this book. A conversation my husband had with me, on numerous occasions was, "Bonnie, write a book! A lot of people could benefit from you sharing your experience in marriage matters and rearing children." What CC said went in one ear and out the other. I was hearing him and not taking the matter seriously.

One day, I was at my husband's job; and one of his coworkers, a friend of ours, unexpectedly said to me, "You should write a book!" It blew my mind to hear out of someone else's mouth confirmation of what CC had been encouraging me to do. Then it seemed like I heard the same suggestion, to write a book, often from unexpected people at unexpected times. Finally, some tragic events got my attention, prompted me, and changed me forever. I will forever remember the service when God directed my Pastor to call me to the altar. There at the altar, I received my assignment from God. Pastor said, "You thought it would be music! But, God said write a book! *When Heaven Holds the Destiny of Your Child* ... Pray and fast that what you share will be able to help others!"

An inspirational e-mail from my son, Quinton, helped as well.

From Q:
April 8, 2010
10:08 p.m.

"Just to encourage you, there are a lot of people anxiously awaiting your book . . ."

10:11 p.m.

"A Legacy of Love . . ." not sure if you had a title in mind already.

This book, *Legacy of Love,* is an opportunity for my family and me to share portions of our life story with all humanity. Our hope is that it will help, inspire, motivate, and encourage all those who read it. Our life story is not a work of fiction . . . it is real. Journey with us and allow us to share with you how blessed we are, how good God is, and how great His love is for us . . . always!

DEVOTION

My Prayer
Dear God,

I bless your name. I give you all the glory. You alone are worthy of all the praise. Thank you for your goodness. Thank you for your kindness. Thank you for your blessings through the years. Thank you for your blessings right now. Thank you, God, for the manifold blessings that are to come. I love you, Lord. I declare that there is none like you. You are mighty, wonderful, awesome, faithful, kind, loving, and true. I love you. Thank you for loving me. I am so unworthy of your great love, but you love me anyway.

Thank you, Lord. Please help me to be all that you would have me to be. Forgive me for every thought, action, or inaction that was not pleasing unto you. Forgive me for all my sins and transgressions. Lord, I don't want anything or anyone to hinder my cry from reaching you. Help me to walk upright and become more and more like you. Lord, please bless my family. Bless the Connie and Shirley Sawyer family. Bless the Melvin and Mamie Downing family. Bless the Connie and Bonnie Sawyer family. Bless believers worldwide. Everywhere and according to your will, heal, deliver and set free. Empower, equip, and enable every believer to be a light and share the gospel of Jesus Christ. Use us to carry forth your purpose and your plan so that you get the glory.

I love you, Jesus. Thank you for all your blessings. Thank you for new mercies each morning. I trust you with my life. I give every care and concern into your care and keeping. My faith looks up to you. I believe that every promise in the Bible is mine. I believe. Have your way and let your perfect will be done. In Jesus' name, I pray. Amen.

SCRIPTURE

Here are divine instructions concerning love. Please keep reading!

I Corinthians 13

¹ Though I speak with the tongues of men and of angels, and have not charity, I am become as sounding brass, or a tinkling cymbal.

² And though I have the gift of prophecy, and understand all mysteries, and all knowledge; and though I have all faith, so that I could remove mountains, and have not charity, I am nothing.

³ And though I bestow all my goods to feed the poor, and though I give my body to be burned, and have not charity, it profiteth me nothing.

⁴ Charity suffereth long, and is kind; charity envieth not; charity vaunteth not itself, is not puffed up,

⁵ Doth not behave itself unseemly, seeketh not her own, is not easily provoked, thinketh no evil;

⁶ Rejoiceth not in iniquity, but rejoiceth in the truth;

[7] Beareth all things, believeth all things, hopeth all things, endureth all things.

[8] Charity never faileth: but whether there be prophecies, they shall fail; whether there be tongues, they shall cease; whether there be knowledge, it shall vanish away.

[9] For we know in part, and we prophesy in part.

[10] But when that which is perfect is come, then that which is in part shall be done away.

[11] When I was a child, I spake as a child, I understood as a child, I thought as a child; but when I became a man, I put away childish things.

[12] For now we see through a glass, darkly; but then face to face: now I know in part; but then shall I know, even as also I am known.

[13] And now abideth faith, hope, charity, these three; but the greatest of these is charity.

CHAPTER 1

The Beginning of the Legacy of Love

Wow! So, where do I go from here? I have made many attempts to put on paper a little of my life story. I want to share who I am, share things that I have been through, and help others. I have hesitated because I did not want to bore anybody to tears. As I give you a peek into my life (or should I say our lives), I hope to share with you the joys as well as some hard times that produced, molded, and shaped the Connie and Bonnie Sawyer family. Trust me! We are blessed! I thank God for His favor upon my family. Many who know our family may be curious as to how we made it. It is no secret— God in our lives makes all the difference.

James 1:2-4 encourages us to count it all joy. Therefore, when I reflect back on my life, I understand that I must recognize my tests and trials as well as my triumphs. Not only must I recognize them, but I must also consider and thank God for the good and the not so good. I am a firm believer that God can use what we endure to shape us into what and who He wants us to be.

I am passionate about many things. I learned that if you do the same thing for twenty-one days, it becomes a habit. A habit can be good or bad. I like to read *Our Daily Bread*. Sometimes, I skip days. So, maybe it has not become something that I habitually read. However, it has been a blessing in my life. I often use the phrase "gold nugget" when referring to insightful information and truths.

That is what I consider *Our Daily Bread* to be - a little book filled with golden nuggets of God's truth. Throughout this book, I will scatter gold nuggets as I tell my story. My hope is that all who read this book will understand the following:

- God must always be first. (Matthew 6:33)
- We must believe and love. (John 3:16; 13:34-35)
- Tithes and offerings release the abundant blessings of God. (Malachi 3:8–12)
- We must trust God with everything. (Proverbs 3:5-6)
- We must have faith. (Hebrews 11:1)
- We must fast and pray. (Matthew 17:20-21)
- We must praise! (Psalm 34:1-3)

It was intentional that I only shared where the scriptures were found. I hope your curiosity is peaked and you will search the scriptures for yourself, read the entire verses, and be empowered. Spend quality time daily with the Lord and it will make a difference in the quality of your life. In fact, we live in a time when people are so busy and have little time to spare for spiritual things. I find myself grabbing the gold nuggets of God's Word and empowering myself. I believe that there is more that God wants me to do and I pray that I fulfill his plan for my life. I truly desire to please Him in all that I do and all that I say.

I want to share with you a truly inspirational entry from *Our Daily Bread*. On March 28, 2010, [1]Paul Van Gorder wrote about the topic "God Needs You!" What he wrote influenced me for the better. I want to share some excerpts.

For His triumphal entry into Jerusalem, Jesus chose a donkey to serve as His royal transportation. His disciples were instructed to say, "The Lord has need of it" (Mark 11:3). Isn't

---

1   Paul Van Gorder, Our Daily Bread, © 2010 by RBC Ministries, Grand Rapids, MI. Reprinted by permission. All rights reserved.

it astounding that the Son of God should use such lowly means to accomplish His purposes? Alexander MacLaren commented on this: "Christ comes to us in like fashion, and brushes aside all our convenient excuses. He says, 'I want you, and that is enough.'"

Think of it! The Creator of the universe needs us and desires to fit us into His eternal design! Though all-powerful and not dependent on any creature, He has chosen to carry out His plans through lowly human instruments.

Someone once asked Francis of Assisi how he was able to accomplish so much. He replied, "This may be why: The Lord looked down from heaven and said, 'Where can I find the weakest, littlest man on earth?' Then He saw me and said, 'I've found him. I will work through him, and he won't be proud of it. He'll see that I am only using him because of his insignificance.'"

You may be small in your own eyes, but God has need of you!

Now, at the very bottom of the page, there is always a maxim. On this date (3/28/10), it read, "God is looking for ordinary people for extraordinary work."

I consider myself one of the ordinary people God will use for extraordinary work. It is a blessing to be alive. You might ask the question, "Why?" Let me tell you this small testimony from my mother's life. She told me about an accident she had. All of the details are fuzzy now in my old age. Oh, how I wish I could remember all of the details. As much as I can remember, she said she was about four years old. Somehow, not listening, following somebody, or something, a car hit her.

The accident was so devastating. Someone used newspaper or some other material to cover her up. Thank God, someone saw that covering moving and realized that there was still breath in the body of that little girl lying in the street. If my mom had not survived that accident, I would not be here. Thank God for His grace and mercy. I am here, and it is all because of His grace and mercy. Thank God, for the angels that watched over my mom that day.

So, you can understand why the entry from *Our Daily Bread* affected me greatly. If God needs me, then He could not allow the one who would birth me into this world to die at an early age. He protected her and the future me. Why did God do it? He had a purpose for my life. Maybe just sharing that will help you understand why I had to write this little book so very much. I feel insignificant, yet purpose is upon me. Hence, my early excuses to leave my story unwritten became void. I press on daily now because I allow Philippians 4:13 to fuel my mind, my heart, and my soul. It reads, "I can do all things through Christ which strengtheneth me." I triumph because Christ enables me, and He gets all the glory.

Who I Am: Bonnie Nadine Downing Sawyer

I am the youngest of nine children. My parents, Melvin, Sr. and Mamie Downing, had seven boys and two girls. My siblings' names are as follows: Melvin, Jr., Edward, Sr., Naomi, Joseph, Sr., Elmore, Samuel, Charles, and Emmitt, Sr. As you can see, the order of births was two boys, my sister, five boys, and then me. It tickles me when I think about all the names they bestowed upon my sister. Even before marriage, she had four names. Maybe they thought she would be the only girl, so they named her after all those special family members, just in case. My oldest three siblings were born while my parents lived in Norfolk, Virginia. The middle three were born while my parents lived in the Crestwood area of Chesapeake, Virginia, and the last three children were born while my parents lived on Fernwood Farms Road in Chesapeake, Virginia.

There is no way that I can omit my siblings by love, who have had a great impact upon my life. I will love you always Starr, Joyce,

Charles, Marcella, Ruby, Kim, Eartha, and Allyson. That's just on the Downing side. On the Sawyer side, understand that I will love you always Esther, Randy, Glenn, Sandra, Maurice, Marnita, Aaron, Jean, Lorietta, Marietta, Al, John, Joice, and Shirl. Also, I want to express appreciation for all my nieces and nephews. I don't want to leave anyone out. Family Always Matters (FAM)! God has truly blessed and I am forever grateful.

Now back to my upbringing. Home for my entire upbringing was Fernwood Farms Road. Many neighbors will always be special to me. I ate pizza for the first time at my next-door neighbor's home. My father, by choice, never tasted pizza his whole life. The granddaughter of my neighbor on the other side was the musician for one of the gospel groups of which I was a participant. My father would not allow me to visit everybody's house. Right now, I can envision those he would allow me to visit. He was very selective. I did not understand then, but now I understand. In his own way, and to the best of his ability, he was just trying to protect me. All the children knew they were welcome to come and play basketball, football, horseshoes, and softball in our huge backyard. Mom and Dad knew how to punish us even without using the switch.

Don't get me wrong, they did not spare the rod and spoil the child. However, imagine a softball game going on in your own back yard and you are on punishment or you have to leave the game because of curfew. Whew! So, I'm looking out of the window and wishing I was in the backyard with the action. I remember the times the neighborhood children would come and ask for permission to play in the backyard. They got permission. Sometimes, I could join the fun and sometimes not. I guess we had the "playground" yard. Children came from far and near to make up the teams for the games.

Remembering My Parents

As I said before, my dad had very strict boundaries for me. I know now that it was because he loved me. I guess it rubbed off on me. When my children wanted to ride their bikes down the street, it was my turn to be nervous. Q would say something like,

"Ma, we'll be OK! You think between here and there a bear is gonna jump out and get us." We would all laugh. They would ride to their destination, return safely, and all would be well. However, not too long ago, my neighbor across the street saw a bear in his yard. I looked out of my window one day and saw a wild boar cut across my yard. We've killed a lot of snakes in and out of the house. Grandma Shirley saw a bear in her back yard. Hum, maybe my concerns were real after all. One thing for sure, I know that God protected us down through the years.

Dad worked hard to take care of his family and provide for us. He was a workaholic. I really do not remember spending a lot of time with him. He left early many mornings and got home late at night. I see now that what inspired my dad was a deep sense of responsibility to provide for his family. He was committed to utilizing as many hours in the day as it would take to accomplish that goal. There were times that he worked so hard and so long that I did not see him for many days in a row.

Though dad was strict, I know he loved me and wanted the very best for me, which included me having a relationship with Christ. My mother and father instilled in me and cultivated my faith. Through their lifestyle, I was able to see faith in action. This, in turn, brought me at an early age into understanding that I needed to give my life to Christ and be accountable to Him. When I was in second grade, about seven or eight years old, I accepted Jesus as my Savior. My father preached a sermon about the fact that you cannot serve two masters. You have to love one and hate the other. His scripture text may have been Matthew 6:24. I believe it was at that moment that I truly made an attempt in my young life to live for the Lord and be different.

I believe a true legacy of love endures and sustains, when there is a relationship with God (who is love). My initial faith in Christ truly helped to begin the legacy of love in my life, which extends now to my children.

Gold nugget: From my own experience, I can safely say that we must nurture our children in the Word of God at an early age. It will make an impact. You can instill truth, values, morals, etc.

in them that will last a lifetime. In Proverbs 22:6, the Bible says, "Train up a child in the way he should go: and when he is old, he will not depart from it." It is the foundation for a legacy of love.

Perhaps, you could classify me today as a reclaimed backslider. Whew! God did not give up on me. I remember the sermon that touched my young, tender heart, yet I strayed away from God when I was a little older. It is so true that God loves with an everlasting love. I could list all the sins that I did not commit; but, oh, I did some crazy things! I am so thankful that my parents took me to church. I'm so glad they prayed for me.

My earliest memories of my mother (Mamie) include observing her being the greatest mom in the world. When I was growing up, she was there in the home. During my preschool years, mom was a homemaker. As the youngest of nine living children, I had days when it was just the two of us at home. Wherever she was, I was close by. When I saw her eating or snacking on something, I asked for some. She asked me one day, "Bonnie, if I was eating horse would you want some?"

"Yes, ma'am!" was my reply.

I saw my mom live out her faith. She was kind, soft spoken, dedicated to her family, and a woman of endurance. She was my earliest role model. Even when she was mistreated, I never saw her return evil for evil. She always loved with agape love. I believe she tried her best to protect and take care of me.

Although Ma (Shirley) and Da (Connie, Sr.) are not my birth parents, they have always entreated me like a daughter. They are a loving couple. Ma and Da shared their home with us the first nine months of our marriage. I will be forever grateful for their kindness.

Their relationship was very different from what I observed in my home. For example, one of the first times I visited, they were in the living room watching TV with the family. Someone had popped popcorn (the old-fashioned way, not in the microwave), and Da was on the couch with his head on Ma's lap. It may seem insignificant; but it was major for me. I'm a romantic at heart and not only could I see the love, I could feel it. Even after a full day of work in the home for Ma and work on the job for Da, there was time to unwind, relax, talk, laugh, and enjoy being together as a family.

It is important to take care of what you have and keep it clean. I did not have a wood heater growing up. We used oil. I found out that having a wood heater and burning wood was messy. Dealing with the wood caused wood chips to accumulate. Sometimes Ma would come by, and the woodpile had caused a big mess on the porch. Ma would say, "Bonnie, I'm going to town. When I come back again, have these chips swept up." I would reply, "Yes, ma'am." Sweeping up wood chips was new to me and not a favorite task, but I did it. Out of obedience, I did what she asked of me. She never told me exactly what time she would be by. However, with urgency, I did what she asked.

Others helped and influenced my becoming who I am today. I thank God again for my parents. I am also grateful for my relatives, teachers, pastors, neighbors, friends, and others, who spoke, read, taught, and lived out the Word of God before me. In my early formative years, my mom and dad walked out their faith before me. How blessed I am to have been so fortunate. It is a great gift to give a child a safe, secure, and Christian environment in which to grow. Even with all the care and protection they gave, bad things happened to me. I know for a fact that it only takes a quick moment, naïveté, and curiosity to strip a child of their innocence. Truly, the good outweighed the bad. Overall, my parents were very strict and perhaps that kept worse things from happening to me.

Gold nugget: It is a good thing when parents place the fear of God in their children. Some children today fear no one and nothing.

While growing up, maybe I took some things for granted. As I reflect back, I now realize how very blessed I was. I analyzed something as simple as filling out information asking for my address, my mom's address, and my dad's address. Growing up all the addresses were the same. What a blessing for me. We live in a day and age when this is not always commonplace.

Remembering My Education and Engagement

For my early education, I attended Crestwood Elementary School and Crestwood Junior High School. I remember much of the change that accompanied the desegregation of public schools. My father was very active in the National Association for the Advancement of Colored People (NAACP) during that time. I attended and graduated from Great Bridge High School in 1976. Norfolk State University was my college of choice. I completed three semesters of study there. My major was Accounting. Twenty years later, when my baby started kindergarten, I re-entered the classroom. Upon completion of two years at College of the Albemarle (COA) in Elizabeth City, North Carolina, I received my Associate's degree with an emphasis in music. In 1998, I graduated from COA, and in 2001, I received my diploma of completion from the Church of God In Christ (COGIC) Academy of Greater North Carolina.

Something very momentous happened the summer before my senior year in, 1975. I met the love of my life, CC. I received an award to attend something like a Governor's Page. My dad said that I could not go. I was very disappointed. Then, the pastor's wife of the church we attended sponsored me to go on the church's summer youth retreat. My dad said that I could go. It was on this trip I met CC, fell in love with him, and the rest truly is history.

I remember standing at the window of my parent's home on Fernwood Farms Road, waiting for my beau to come see me. He never disappointed me. Such a love I had and have for this man. Romans 8:28 rings true once again. What if I had gone to the school function and not gone to the Youth Congress? What would my life be like if I had never met CC? Well, it all came together. We have been married now for thirty-nine years.

Many things happened in my life before 1975. Much has happened since 1975 when I first met my husband. I now have children and grandchildren. I smile when I write this. The family is growing. Love is in the air! Love is in the heart! Love is all around! I know that in God's own time, our family will continue to increase by love, marriage, and births.

CHAPTER 2

The Preparation for the Legacy of Love

I truly believe God, in His mercy, prepared me for my marriage. At the time, I did not realize that fact. As I look back over my life and see the things that I had to endure, I see it all so clear now. It was hard. I did not want my life to be like it was; but, it was a blessing in disguise. The things I endured contributed to the legacy of love that I would demonstrate and pass on to my children.

For example, when I was growing up, our hot water heater stopped working. I do not know how or why. I just know that we were not able to turn on the faucet and get hot water. Knowing as I know now, all that was required was to take out the old hot water heater, replace it, and have the new one installed. Nevertheless, we heated every bit of hot water we used on the stove. That's what we did.

Marriage, the early years

Well, when I got married, I did not have running water. We originally had an old hand pump at the sink in the kitchen. Every bit of water I used, I had to pump it up from the well. Sometimes the connection was lost, and I had to prime the pump. I learned to have a little water set aside for this purpose. In addition, if I wanted to use hot water, I heated it on the cook stove. I just see the preparation in it all. I never knew that after my marriage I would be in a situation such as this.

About nine months after my marriage, I moved into these living conditions. We moved in with a kind woman, named Ms. Sue. She had suffered several strokes. It was good for us to live with her, so she would not live alone. It was good for her to have others in the house with her in case something happened. Her daughter Edna lived maybe one-mile right down the street. Ms. Sue wanted to be home. We have all heard the saying, "There's no place like home." Well, I am sure that's how Ms. Sue felt.

Ms. Edna and Ma were good friends. Ms. Edna is now deceased. We will be forever grateful for her generosity to our family. Connie, Jr., baby, Connie, III, and I went to stay with Ms. Sue and Ms. Edna was comforted knowing that her mom was not living alone. All Ms. Edna had to go on was her friendship with Ma. She trusted that friendship and the integrity of Ma to allow CC and me to be caregivers and company for her mother. Ma had gotten to know me better over the nine months that I stayed with them.

This transition would allow me to ease into being the lady of the house. Now, do not get me wrong. I respected Ms. Sue. However, she could not sweep, scrub, dust, cook, or wash clothes. All those household duties were my responsibility. We had a great understanding and mutual respect. Her left side was weak because of the strokes. When she walked, that left foot would drag a little. Any time of the day, you could see her exercising that weaker left arm. She was actually doing physical therapy to straighten that arm to a different position other than it's natural L–shape close to her upper body. I mentioned all of that because, even in her weakened state, I felt so safe with her in the house. She never left the house. Once she got up in the morning and got dressed, she would come to her sitting room and sit by the window. Trust me; she saw whatever went on in and around her home and the neighbors'. She never left home. She was always there. For three to four years of my marriage, she was there every day. When she was gone from this earth forever, I was devastated. I felt like, she is gone, now who is going to protect me when CC is not here?"

Learning Humility and Responsibility

I thank God for my humble beginning. I thank God for the hard times that molded and shaped me. When we lived with Mom and Pop Sawyer, we had to pay them a certain amount each month. They were teaching us responsibility. They did not raise their nine children drinking Kool-Aid every night. Having Kool-Aid was a treat for special occasions. I found out through experience that something as simple as drinking Kool-Aid could be costly over time. Even with us giving them what money they asked for, they did not drain or deplete us. They imparted wisdom to us.

Because we listened, when we moved with Ms. Sue, we had saved about $2,000 dollars. This money was for rainy days, for hard times, for those unexpected things that just pop up. The light bill became our responsibility when we moved in with Ms. Sue. It was about $11. Is God good or what? We had other financial obligations of course, but I just wanted to pause and thank God for that $11 electric bill that eventually increased because more people used electricity in the home. While it lasted, it was great.

Now, Ms. Sue's home was a humble dwelling. As I stated before, I did not have running water, a bathroom, and many of the comforts that we take for granted. Nevertheless, I was happy to be there. I was married to my high school sweetheart and so in love. He told me early on in the marriage that he appreciated me enduring the things that I endured. "I don't know if other ladies would do what you do," he said. I am grateful, however, that today, we have three bathrooms, running water, washer, dryer, a central air/heating system, and all the comforts that our blessed home can afford.

How did we make it all those years before? Initially, we had a wood stove for our main heat source. Eventually, we added electric baseboard heaters when we renovated. Now anybody who knows anything about wood heat knows that it gives wonderful heat that warms you down to your bones. It saturates. Once that heater gets going, you have to wait until the fire dies down. You have to open a window, crack the door, or something to cool down. All of my family has fond memories of the wood heater top loaded with Sunday, Thanksgiving, or Christmas dinner. In several pots and pans would be macaroni and cheese, collard greens, yams, turkey, stuffing, etc. It served as the warming station many days, not just the holidays. You could walk up to the wood stove, lift the top off the greens, and hear the sound of the pot simmering. The aroma of the food was all throughout the house. It was heavenly!

It was my upbringing and the challenging times from the earliest days of my marriage that God used to prepare me for raising a family in challenging situations. I thank God for the process.

CHAPTER 3

The Process of the Legacy of Love:
How We Made It as a Family

W hen I got married to CC, I was the happiest woman alive. I was happy and scared at the same time. I had never been married before. We all experience apprehension when we venture into the unknown. I wanted to be a good wife and mother, and all I had to pull on was what I had seen in my own mother and what I was observing in my new mother-in-law. As I reflect back on the early days of being a wife and mother, I remember on a sunny day in the year of 1978, I could see the sun shining through my kitchen walls.

I remember the hand pump in my kitchen, which provided us with water. There was no bathroom. There was no running water. I remember the wringer washer that I filled with water from the hand pump. I remember the rinse tub that I used to rinse the clothes and doubled as the bathtub to bathe my babies.

When I remember the times before we had a bathroom, before we had running water, when we had to use the hand pump inside my kitchen to get all the water that we used, I feel like giving God praise. I was thankful when I finally did not have to use the hand pump to get water. By the way, the water from the hand pump was excellent. Because of all the effort it took to wash clothes, I kept them washed up. It would be out of the ordinary to come into my home and see piles of dirty clothes. Not having the most modern conveniences was not an excuse. I used what I had because it was what I had to use.

Work What You Have

It is important to do all that you can today. John 9:4 says, "I must work the works of him that sent me, while it is day: the night cometh, when no man can work." Also, Ecclesiastes 9:10 says, "Whatsoever thy hand findeth to do, do it with thy might; for there is no work, nor device, nor knowledge, nor wisdom in the grave, whither thou goest." In other words, it is not good to procrastinate. Procrastination leads to lost opportunities and incomplete assignments. Procrastination actually allows perfectly good time to slip through your fingers. Procrastination is breeding ground for the coulda', woulda', shoulda' blues.

I am blessed. As I share more about how we made it, understand that God in our lives makes all the difference. When I look at the successful things that have happened in my family, I see the blessings and favor of God. He did it. He made it possible. Our lives could have turned out so differently. God favored all of us and showered down grace and mercy. I am thankful. However, we had to work at it. We had to learn how to work what we had in order to get to where we wanted to be. God was certainly with us, but we needed to work at our marriage and rearing our children. We needed to work and work TOGETHER!

Ecclesiastes 4: 9-12 says, "Two are better than one; because they have a good reward for their labour. For if they fall, the one will lift up his fellow: but woe to him that is alone when he falleth; for he hath not another to help him up. Again, if two lie together, then they have heat: but how can one be warm alone? And if one prevail against him, two shall withstand him; and a threefold cord is not quickly broken." As a family, we must stay close. We do need one another to survive. As I continue my story, you will understand why work, along with my faith in God was necessary. The continual involvement and support of others were vital in the beginning days, the days of being a wife, and the days of becoming the mother of eventually nine children. Now, back to my story.

Well, using an old-fashioned wringer washer and rinse tub required keeping up with the weather. For instance, hanging out clothes during the raining season took some planning. If I did not bring in the clothes before the rain started, they could end up on the line for more than one day. There was no electric dryer during the early years. When they stayed out in the rain, I would think of it as an extra rinse cycle. However, if the rain, falling so intensely, caused mud to splash up, I would have to rewash the clothes. I never liked going to the Laundromat. I would rather wash clothes at home with the wringer washer and hang clothes on the clothesline … even in the snow. In the winter, the clothes would freeze dry and could be thawed out and ironed at the same time on the top of the wood heater.

When it was bath time, my four oldest, Connie, III, Joshua, Q, and Portia were all small enough to fit in the rinse tub at the same time. I had no bathtub, but I used what I had. I pumped the water, heated it, put it in the tub, cooled it off to the right temperature, and bathed my babies. All in the bath, out one by one, and each one wrapped in a towel. Children, do you remember the chant … Choo, choo, choo, choo, choo … stop …! You all would all stop, do a little dance, and then start all over again with your after-bath chant.

Have you ever heard of the saying, "Is your glass half full or half empty?" Well, the essence behind that statement is simply perspective. Are you optimistic or full of negativity? With all that I had to endure, I could have opted to become bitter, despondent, and full of negativity. I chose to focus on my blessings, thank God, praise God, and wait for my change.

Gold nugget: Thinking positive will keep you happy, encouraged, and motivated. Waiting is a part of living. Many things that you pray for will come, just not always immediately. As an individual, you decide how you will spend your waiting time. Will you be miserable or still praising God for being God? Trust me. The praising option is the best way to go.

Make Difficult Choices

Through the hard times, the love flowed so freely. God allowed the hardships so that our lives would not be superficial. God truly made our life at home into a legacy of love and not stuff. In our home, smiles were abundant, and we were thankful. It is awesome how God would take a newly married, struggling couple and just ease us into the realities of life. Furthermore, God met every need. My husband worked hard and understood the difficulties in our situation at the time. He offered me praise and encouragement through it all. In my heart, I knew that I loved him; and if this was all he could provide, then so be it.

This legacy of love is a continuing process for our lives. For example, the kitchen can be an amazing place. In the kitchen, not only are cooking skills learned, but also life lessons learned. We were probably in the kitchen one day preparing a meal when my mother-in-law presented a challenge to me. This conversation happened before we moved in with Ms. Sue.

"Now, Bonnie are you going to be a career woman or are you going to be a homemaker?"

I had to make this difficult decision. I could work and thus have more money; or, I could choose to stay at home. By not working, I would endure the difficulties that could arise with one income upholding bills and expenses of parenthood. Nevertheless, I chose the latter.

This choice placed our family in a place of total dependence on God's provision. We appreciated one another in a greater fashion. We could not hide behind amenities in the home; we learned to live with one another. Investing love, time, and energy into family, spouse, and the life and upbringing of children would come at a cost. However, you cannot attach a dollar value to it. Other difficult decisions awaited us, but making them and accepting the consequences of those decisions aided in the overall process. I believe that the blessings upon my family are a direct result of the decision that I made. My homemaker career is different from the path of my mom (Mamie) and Ma (Shirley). I stand corrected. Maybe my homemaker career is similar to theirs in some aspects.

I did work, occasionally, but whatever jobs I did when the children were very young, I based it inside of my home. Particularly, teaching beginner piano and working for Watermark, an arts and crafts co-operative that allowed me to do crafts in my home, submit them by the deadline, and receive payment for the finished product. Through the Cooperative, I learned to weave baskets, to design my own baskets, to make dolls, to paint buttons and to produce other crafts. The children actually helped me with the crafts. Remember, you have to work what you have.

Gold nugget: Yes, I have made mistakes in decisions and choices. However, overall, to stay at home with my children was the right choice for me. My hat is off to those women who have to work outside the home. However, what needs to happen inside the home must happen as well. We have heard the saying: "Charity begins at home and then spreads abroad." Somehow, someway, you must balance home and work.

CHAPTER 4

The Development of the Legacy of Love

I have said it before and I will say it again, I love my husband dearly. He has always provided for our family and been a father to our children. He understands his God-given role in our family. There could be no true development of the legacy of love in the CbSawyer (Connie and Bonnie Sawyer) family without his leadership as a godly husband and father. Before I continue to go in detail, I want to give you the opportunity to hear from the rock of this family; my husband, Connie Sawyer, Jr., with an inside view.

Connie, Jr.'s Inside View

It is quite a challenge when I think about where to start describing my ride through these years. As you read each page of this book, remember that I was impacted, and in many cases, "the impact" of it all. Some of you might say, "What do you mean?" Well, as the priest of my family, it was up to me to set the tone for the direction that my family would take. No matter how things seemed or felt, I had to remember what the Bible instructed me as a father and follow those instructions. When the many questions and choices came up concerning the children, I had to consult the Bible for direction. I am not saying that it was always easy to do this. In fact, it was often very difficult, but I tried to keep what the Bible says as my focus. It worked. I want to say right at the beginning that I am so Godly proud of each one of our children (and their spouses) and what they have accomplished. It gives me great joy to talk about them.

How did it all begin? When Bonnie and I were married, we did not have very much. In fact, we had almost nothing. We got married February 4, 1978. I graduated from Elizabeth City State University in December 1979, and in January 1980, I began working for the General Accounting Office at a beginning salary of $6,800 per year. Living with my parents, we began this marriage journey, not really knowing exactly where it would lead. However, we knew that if we followed and trusted in God, He would direct us. We also knew that we loved each other and that we could overcome any obstacles that we would encounter. After about nine months of being married, we left my parent's home and moved with our first child to our current location, to live with Ms. Sue, the mother of Mrs. Edna Aydlett. Ms. Sue was a great blessing to us. We lived with her in a two-bedroom house, with no running water or indoor plumbing. All she charged us for rent was the increase in her electric bill, which was usually less than about $10 per month.

Can you imagine living in a four-room house with a wife and four children and no bathroom or indoor plumbing? Add to that another child on the way. I worked in a professional organization, and it was often difficult to talk about where I lived. I was very reluctant to invite others to our home because we didn't have a bathroom or indoor plumbing. Then again, we were very happy together. I began our marriage by teaching my family to live by the Word of God. After about three years of marriage and living in the house with Ms. Sue, God called her home. We really miss her. We were able to buy the house from her son, and this gave us a start. Realizing that I wanted to provide more for Bonnie and the kids, I began making plans to add to the house. Thank God, I learned the skills of carpentry, plumbing, and electricity at an early age. My prayer was that I could build onto the house while also living in it and continuing to work. Well, I began a building project to add about 1,200 square feet to the house.

This would give us a master bedroom with bathroom, another bedroom, a utility room, kitchen, bathroom, and a large living room. God answered my prayer. I was able to drive to Virginia Beach, VA for work, and after work, I would come home and work on the addition. After many long days and a two- or three-month burnout period of no work, I was able to complete the project. A special thank-you goes out to my brothers Glenn and Maurice, along with the crew of Sawyer's Home Improvement, for their assistance in helping me complete the project after my burnout period. My goal was to complete the addition before Bonnie came home from the hospital after Crystal was born. When she came home, she moved into her new master bedroom.

Twenty-five years after the first addition to the house, we (now nine children, some with spouses and their own children) were sitting in the family room, and there did not seem to be enough room. I told my family that I was going to add another room to the house. They really did not understand what I had in mind. I added approximately 1,500 square feet to the house. During the construction period, which took about two years, God impressed upon me that our home would be a place of refuge. It now serves as a place where people come for shelter, comfort, fellowship, and a good meal.

As I strove to provide a physical place for my family to live, I also tried to set a standard of holy living that we would abide by. It was often difficult to tell the children that they could not do certain things or go certain places, but my responsibility was to raise them in the fear and admonition of God, not to be their friend. As the children got older, they did not always agree with my decisions, but they respected them. Today, each of my children respects me for being a father to them, and now, we can be friends. There is so much more that I could say, but I'll let Bonnie continue.

Legacy of Love Begins with Honesty

All I can say is, "Didn't you enjoy hearing from my wonderful husband?" Alright, let me continue. After the birth of our first son, the doctor told me that I did such a good job that I should have a baby every year. I really did not set out to fulfill that advice (seeing the grand total would be nine). I remember my mother advising me not to holler during delivery. I remember asking the nurses if I had to holler like the other woman in the room. I remember talking to the caregivers and asking many questions and looking in the mirror during his birth. The birth was amazing. After the birth of our first son, CC realized that he could accompany me in the delivery room. He was there for all the rest and would have been for the first if we had only known. Having CC with me in the delivery room from then on, made a wonderful difference.

Children are a gift straight from God. To be a parent is a great honor. Rearing the children should never be a chore or drudgery. When that happens, parents, please search your heart. All nine children were born within a twelve and a half year time span (August 1978 – February 1991). We treasure our family. However, the first child came under some interesting circumstances. I thank God for loving me with His agape love. It is always best to do things and live life according to the Word of God. However, when you are young and in love, sometimes things happen. I have been afraid. I have been scared. I have been unsure how my future would turn out. I felt like running away. Tell me, how do you run away from yourself?

I am eternally thankful for my family members and my husband's family members that helped me and helped us through difficult times. Where would we be today if it had not been for their love, forgiveness, and assistance? Agape love is awesome. I wrestled with whether to include certain information about my past. However, I believe it is important that I expose my wounds. In other words, where I am today is not how I started.

I had to have a truth talk with my oldest son. I cannot remember how old he was. Yes, his question took me by surprise. He did not ask in any manner of disrespect. He was just seeking truth and understanding. His question on this particular day was something like, "Ma, I thought it took nine months for a baby to be born. Y'all got married in February, and I was born in August." (I told you the first child came with an interesting circumstance.) Yeah! I had a choice, to tell the truth, or just say something to take his mind off his question. Whew! I really do not remember all that I said to him that day. However, I told him the truth.

Among other things, I first let him know that I was pregnant with him before I got married. I shared with him that sometimes this happens and the two people never get married. I told him how blessed I was that his daddy did marry me. I took the time to explain to him how important it is to do things God's way. Two people should get married first and then have the children. Someone told me that I should have brought up the subject of premature babies. If I had told him that, it would have left him with the impression that he was a premature baby. He was not premature! He was full term and lying to him, honestly, never crossed my mind at that moment. Just as I am being transparent right now, that is how I am by nature. I told my son the truth. We have never had that conversation again. I respect my son, and I believe he respects me because I told him the truth then and even now.

Somebody else out there can relate to my story. Now, how can I look down on others with a similar history? How can I not have compassion for those who are going through similar things that I went through? Some of my children have gone through the same similar pathway. Do I condone it (the choice to interact as a married couple before marriage)? No! Just as God forgives, we must forgive and love that individual to life.

Gold nugget: We live in a day whereby we must teach our children. Talk to them truthfully and encourage them to do things in God's way. I cannot give guarantees on exactly how things will turn out. However, if we do all that we know to do and do what we do according to God's Word, we will be victorious.

While growing up, I satisfied my curiosity by reading books, magazines, etc. In fact, that's how I learned about the 'birds and bees'. I don't recall having in-depth conversations about life with my parents. What little I do remember about the conversations is that the conversations were awkward and full of abstract imagery. Parents, we need to be the source of giving our children the truth. We must present the truth clearly. Is it fair to hope that the children will pick up some random magazine or book and learn about life? Furthermore, we must not leave it up to one child to educate another child. If we leave it up to the children, it will be like the blind leading the blind with misguided half-truths and myths. We have to throw modesty to the wind and establish a relationship whereby our children will feel comfortable and free to ask questions and talk to us about anything. We must be willing to help them to the best of our abilities. We must tell them what the Bible says. Parents, you might enter into a conversation that makes you feel uncomfortable. If it will help your child in the end, then press on. If you want to develop and pass on a legacy of love, you must be willing to love them enough to tell them the truth. This type of love will enable you to accomplish things that you never imagined possible. Your child's life and future could be at stake.

Legacy of love develops through Interaction

If you really love your child, take out time with them. Listen to them. Hear what they are saying. Observe them. When you see drastic changes in behavior or school performance, investigate. Sometimes, when they act out, they are crying out for help. Yes, you chastise them. You correct them. Just make sure you get to the root of what the issue is. Always show concern and care. Denial does not make it go away. Burying your head in the sand so that you do not have to look at certain things does not make the issues disappear. Continual interaction is necessary; they need provision as well as supervision.

When the children were sick, I was there. When they had school plays, I could be there. I was able to pick them up after school from sports or band activities most of the time. As I look back over the years, I realize how privileged I was to be there for my children in so many ways. I always felt responsible for the safety and well-being of my children. Even with all that I was able to do,

I still could not have made it without the help of my husband and dear friends who entreated my children as their own. My friends picked up and carried my children along with their own children at times when I was not able. Thank you! Thank you! Thank you!

Parents, know that it is okay not to let your child sleep over at any and everybody's house. You can never really know all that happens behind another person's closed door. I did let my children spend the night away from home. I thought I was wise with my decisions. Then I had to reconsider my choices. Sometimes we have to live and learn the hard way. I let one of my daughters spend the night at a friend's house. When I went to pick her up, some things caught my attention. Yes, a man has the right to be the king of his castle. However, when I walked in and I saw beer and heard profanity, I had to rethink my actions. My daughter did not have to be in that environment. Therefore, I had to make a decision not to place her in it. She did not experience certain things in her home, so she really did not have to be subject to it. When kids are young, they are very impressionable. They will observe and imitate what they observe.

We have to be careful of what we tolerate. I had one son come home from school and spell a curse word. He never said the word, but he spelled it most accurately. I had to let him know immediately that whoever and wherever he got it from, he must not bring it into our home. I told him that he would get the spanking, and whoever he got that knowledge from would probably be home watching TV. I do not remember all that I said but he got the message. Be careful whom you entrust your children with. Protect your children. Listen to your children. Do not subject your children to lifestyle choices that are displeasing to God. If you do, it will grow up in them. They will do ungodly things as children, and they will do ungodly things as adults.

I believe God bestows something very special upon parents. It enables us to tap into situations that could otherwise go undetected. For example, sometimes parents have special soda, candy, whatever that the kids know not to bother. These many years later, I truly cannot remember exactly what it was. Whatever it was, I know it was in the refrigerator. When I found out the guilty son, I believe he got a spanking. I used it as a lesson about stealing. Though it was in the home, you should not take or use something that does not belong to you without asking or permission. I explained that stealing was not right.

The Bible says, "Thou shalt not steal." Then he had to memorize Luke 12:2, "For there is nothing covered that shall not be revealed; neither hid, that shall not be known." What is done in the dark will come to the light. I wanted a word to be with him in case he tried certain things in the future. This word has stuck with him through the years.

We should go to the Word for direction and instruction when we deal with our children. When they ask, "Why?" we should allow the Bible to speak. Train them to believe every promise, every word, and every epistle of the Bible without question.

Legacy of Love demands Discipline

Parents, it is a mistake to try to satisfy every appetite of your children. It is an error to think about your hard upbringing and try to compensate by giving your child every heartfelt desire. A true legacy of love comes with a disciplined approach to parenting and the execution of discipline as a parent. When we try to give them everything and more stuff, it will not satisfy the appetite for more stuff. A humble upbringing is able to give birth to an individual that is thankful and appreciative for life's blessings.

I never thought it was a good idea to do a lot of borrowing. How would you feel if you had to replace something that you could not afford in the first place? Is it a sign of discontent when you borrow? When the children participated in school plays or times of character dress up, I may have borrowed things that I did not have and could not afford to buy for one-time use. In a case like that, it is only fair to impress upon the child how important it is to take very good care of what was loaned to them. Afterward, return it. Always say thank you. Above all else, teach them to be content and happy with what they have.

Acquiring more stuff and things should not be the main agenda. We must not only teach our youth about God, but we must teach them to put God first. God is only happy and satisfied when we put Him first. To put God first should not be up for debate. We must wait, hope, and trust Him to give us what is best. Matthew 6:33 says, "But seek ye first the kingdom of God, and his righteousness; and all these things shall be added unto you." We must obey God's Word. When we approach life outside of God's order, we will become frustrated and fail.

They must know early on that our actions carry consequences. We must teach them that it is important for them to follow rules and guidelines. The danger in getting by when doing evil is that you keep on and cannot stop, or it is too late. They must respect authority and be obedient. Deeds done in the dark will come to the light. The more you get by, the more you keep living on the edge.

People would come and tell me things about my children without me asking. They gave me information in general conversation. They did not tell me to be tattling. It was just a general conversation. Many times, I would confront my child concerning a matter. My conversation would go something like, "Tell me what happened and please tell me the truth. I already know!" Trust me. That was a mercy call. They all knew that discipline was always worse when lying was involved. Even if a spanking was coming, it was always better, to tell the truth.

The Bible says in Proverbs 13:24 "He that spareth his rod hateth his son: but he that loveth him chasteneth him betimes." Proverbs 23:13 says, "Withhold not correction from the child: for if thou beatest him with the rod, he shall not die. A rod here refers to a switch, used for whipping somebody as a punishment. Modern society views any type of corporal (physical) discipline as abuse and barbaric. Parents, we correct our children because we love them. Keep in mind Colossians 3:21, "Fathers, provoke not your children to anger, lest they be discouraged."

Gold nugget: Let me explain also that you should never chastise your child in anger. Do not chastise your child when you are frustrated about something else. Do not abuse your children. I do not believe we should be grabbing them, yanking them, or pointing our fingers in their faces. Our tone of voice needs to be right.

I can never remember my mom doing any of those things (grabbing, yanking, yelling, etc.) to me as I was growing up. I truly respected her and looked up to her. She walked out her faith. My mom was very soft spoken. On the phone, she sounded like a little girl. The Christ-like character in her just radiated out. She was a strong woman with a soft voice and invincible faith. My mom was all of those great things, and she still disciplined me. Daddy talked, too, with that deep voice that put the fear of God into you. And, Daddy did most of the spanking.

Legacy of Love is founded upon the Bible

Developing a legacy of love through parenting, not only takes honesty, interaction, and discipline, but also a foundation of the Word of God as one navigates life and its challenges. In raising our children, we always gave them the Word and explained why we did what we did as parents, from the scriptures. As I give brief excerpts from my life to show how one develops a legacy of love that your children will pass on to future generations, understand that the Word guided us throughout.

As we interact with and discipline our children, we should season instructions with the Word. Why do you do what you do? The answer is in the Word. Why do you act and react the way you do? The answer is in the Word. Why do you say what you say? The answer is in the Word! Mark 8:36 says, "For what shall it profit a man, if he shall gain the whole world, and lose his own soul?"

We should never foster, condone, or excuse sin and inappropriate behavior in our children. We must continually teach our children the Word. When I think about teaching the Word to our children, I think about the ABC Memory Verses developed from the COGIC Sunshine Band. It was always awesome to hear the children recite not only the memory verses from A–Z; but also the chapter and verse of each scripture. Even now, years later, my children remember some, if not all, of these scriptures. The Word is powerful enough to keep, sustain, and maintain us as we go through the tests and trials of life. It helped us as we reared our children in difficult situations.

Think about how life- giving the Word is. What greater gift can you give to a child? It requires memory and discipline to commit scripture to the heart and mind. It is well worth the time, energy, and effort to instill the Word of God into our children. I am a witness that the Word sustained me in life. When I felt like tossing in the towel, the Word says, "And let us not be weary in well doing: for in due season we shall reap, if we faint not." Galatians 6:9

ABC Memory Verses

A - ... **a**ll have sinned, and come short of the glory of God; (Romans 3:23)

B - ... **b**elieve on the Lord Jesus Christ, and thou shalt be saved ... (Acts 16:31)

C – Children, obey your parents in the Lord: for this is right. (Ephesians 6:1)

D - Depart from evil, and do good ... (Psalm 34:14)

E - Even a child is known by his doings ... (Proverbs 20:11)

F - Fear not: for I *am* with thee ... (Isaiah 43:5)

G - ... **G**od is love. (I John 4:8)

H - Honour thy father and thy mother ... (Exodus 20:12)

I - If ye shall ask anything in my name, I will do *it*. (John 14:14)

J - Jesus saith unto him, I am the way, the truth, and the life ... (John 14:6)

K - Keep thy tongue from evil... (Psalm 34:13)

L - **L**ook unto Me, and be ye saved ... (Isaiah 45:22)

M - **M**y son, give me thine heart ... (Proverbs 23:26)

N - **N**o man can serve two masters ... (Matthew 6:24)

O - **O** give thanks unto the LORD; for *He* is good ... (Psalm 118:1)

P - **P**raise ye the LORD: for *it is* good to sing praises unto our God ... (Psalm 147:1)

Q - **Q**uench not the Spirit. (I Thessalonians 5:19)

R - **R**emember the Sabbath day, to keep it holy. (Exodus 20:8)

S - **S**eek ye the LORD while He may be found ... (Isaiah 55:6)

T - ... **t**hou God seest me ... (Genesis 16:13)

U - **U***nto Thee*, O God, do we give thanks ... (Psalm 75:1)

V - ... **V**erily, verily, I say unto you, Whatsoever ye shall ask the Father in my name, He will give *it* you." (John 16:23)

W - **W**hat time I am afraid, I will trust in Thee. (Psalm 56:3)

X - ... e**x**ceeding great and precious promises are given unto us ... (II Peter 1:4)

Y - **Y**e are the light of the world. (Matthew 5:14)

Z - ... be **z**ealous therefore, and repent. (Revelation 3:19)

I will forever be grateful to Grandma Shirley and Grandda Connie for investing love and time into their grandchildren. They worked with their grandchildren at church and outside of the church. The children had to learn the ABC memory verses, other scriptures, parts for skits, as well as songs of faith; all of which the children would travel and bless others with. Thank you, Grandma Shirley and Grandda Connie.

It does take a village to rear a child. God made sure others helped us. A legacy of love demands outside involvement, encouragement, and help. We are so appreciative to all who helped us along the way. Thank you to our parents, grandparents, siblings, aunts, uncles, cousins, neighbors, and friends. Thank you to the teachers, principals, coaches, and advisors who helped to nurture our children.

We made it because of the prayers of our pastors, parents, deacons, missionaries, saints, and friends. For those known/ anonymous gifts of clothes, shoes, coats, and toys given directly or left at my door, we thank you. For the delicious meals, you shared at your table in your home, thank you. For being there, supporting us, and babysitting nine children at one time overnight, thank you. Thank you to the farmers, who allowed us to glean in their fields. Thank you for the scuppernong grapes! For celebrating with us, mourning with us, and loving us to life, thank you.

CHAPTER 5

The Power and Inspiration of the Legacy of Love

Prayer is so important to me. I Thessalonians 5:17 says, "Pray without ceasing." As I reflect on my life, and how this legacy of love developed, I declare that one unseen power behind it all has always been prayer. It took continual, fervent, and sincere prayer to make it. However, God has always been gracious to hear, answer, strengthen, and give me what I need to make it. In the last chapter, I talked about things that helped us as we parented our children. Now I want to talk about the importance of prayer.

Power through Prayer

As a little girl, prayer was important to my family and it certainly was crucial to survival as a wife and mother. Aside from the normal duties that come with parenting, there is one more duty that you cannot neglect. I am witness to its importance. Pray with your children! Many times, when we prayed together as a family, it was the norm for mom, dad, and each child to pray. Granted it made for a sometimes-lengthy prayer time, but it was so worth every minute.

Gold nugget: Parents/Guardians, it will bless you to hear your children pray. It will bring tears to your eyes and joy to your souls. Really, listen to them when they pray. Encourage them to pray. It is true that the family that prays together stays together. It is the power behind the legacy. Our faith, prayer, and worship together at church and home have cemented our family together to make us strong.

Since prayer has shaped and blessed my life, my family and friends understand that I will send up a prayer gladly at any given point in time of the day. It is my delight to do so. They call for prayer when about to board a plane, get on a bus, drive, or while just at their homes. We pray, give God thanks, ask for His forgiveness, tell God how wonderful He is, how much we need Him, how much we appreciate His blessings, and we make our requests known. Philippians 4:6 says, "Be careful for nothing; but in everything by prayer and supplication with thanksgiving let your requests be made known unto God." It is imperative that we give God all that is due Him. Really, how would we feel if all the conversation directed toward us was a request for stuff? How would we feel if we never received a "thank you" for things already done? For praise is the conclusion of every prayer.

In March of 1999, I joined a new church closer to home, led by one of my brothers-in-law, Pastor Glenn Sawyer. One of the services at the church was noonday prayer. Now, I grew up in the church. I have participated in prayer and prayer meetings. However, the church I attended before was one hour away and I had never participated in an established noonday prayer gathering. Therefore, I asked our pastor's wife, "What do you do at noonday prayer?" I really did not know all to do in such a setting. I asked her because I just wanted to make sure I was in order. Her response was something like, "You pray!" Her simple response relieved my concerns. She is so full of wisdom. We sang and prayed, and God blessed mightily.

Partnerships in Prayer

I have also discovered that family prayer time is essential. In fact, I need the prayers of others for mutual strength and encouragement. I know, through the years, that the prayers and intercessions of others brought me through when situations were so challenging that I could not find the words to pray what was in my heart. Some years ago, I responded to a challenge by our pastor to have a prayer partner, become accountable, and seek God early before the enemy has a chance to attack. I started, and then it dwindled off to not praying with my prayer partner at all.

During one service, he asked all the ones who were still actively praying with their prayer partners to stand up. I could not. I did not like that fact. When one sister stood and shared that her prayer partner was her husband, that fact caught my attention. I liked that. Therefore, to be honest, I took things to another level to make sure that one of my prayer partners was my husband.

Gold nugget: A prayer partner holds you accountable daily to prayer. A prayer partner understands how important it is to offer God sacrificial prayer. I phrase it that way because sometimes it is so early in the morning, sometimes the call wakes you up out of a deep sleep, and it is a sacrifice.

I have had three to four prayer partners at one time. Sometimes I have had one prayer partner beep in on the phone while I was praying with another prayer partner. Some calls have been as early as 4:00 a.m. Thank you to all of my current prayer partners. To the ones that I no longer pray with, I thank you for the season that we prayed together. I thank God for my prayer partners through the years. They have been such a blessing in my life.

Praise is the Twin of Prayer

Prayer sustains me. Prayer washes over me and refreshes. I become fortified and stronger because of prayer. My hope is renewed. My faith is renewed. My trust is renewed. However, the twin of prayer is praise. I need both. So, when I can't find the words to pray, I can at least offer God praise as a sign of keeping the faith in difficult situations. Praise to God through songs and instruments helped my family to make it. Prayer and praise are mighty weapons of warfare working together for my good. To conclude this section, I want to share a few testimonies of prayer, which demanded praise in the end. I have many stories I could share, but I chose a few just to give you a glimpse as to why praise is my constant companion.

Every day is a day of thanksgiving. I realize that God has not only spared my life but also my husband, children, and family numerous times through the years. I remember on one occasion, the doctor telling me that they had to do a biopsy on me. I was fearful. I was trying to think of an accurate word to describe my emotions. I was really scared! Yes, I trust God. Nevertheless, I was still scared. One noonday, maybe after prayer, I asked Pastor Glenn Sawyer to pray for me. I do not remember all that I said. He did pray for me immediately. I thanked God for the prayer. My tests results came back benign. Praise God! I tell you, I owe God praise. He has been so good to me.

It could have gone another way. During this time, I had a friend going through the same types of tests. Her tests came back positive. God brought us both through. We are still going forth and giving God the praise. We know that God is a healer and miracle worker. God never fails. After God allows the doctors to do all they know to do, God steps in with His wondrous working power.

Let me give you another testimony of prayer and praise. Often, I think about the accident that my son Q was in. I could be saying that I had nine children, but now I have eight living children. I believe he was in the eleventh grade. Anyway, this particular day, Q and his cousin, Elbert, were on their way to Virginia. The car Q was driving went across the center line on the road, jumped the ditch, hit three trees, and ended up on its side. Elbert climbed out of the sunroof to get to the road for help. I do not think I will ever forget that knock at the door and the cry from a friend that Q had been in an accident. We actually heard about the accident on the radio scanner.

My husband, CC, is a volunteer firefighter and was having back pain on this particular day. Therefore, he decided not to respond to the call when his pager went off. We heard conversation concerning the accident but had no clue it was our son. They had only been gone for a few minutes. They had only traveled approximately five miles. At the scene of the accident, Q was confused and could not remember what had happened. I was frantic. I could not get close to him at the scene of the accident. His dad could get close because he is a volunteer firefighter. His dad rode with him to the hospital in the ambulance. I drove the car over. The trip to the accident scene and the ride to the hospital seemed to take forever.

At the hospital, Q said, "I want granddaddy (Connie, Sr.)!" Grandda Connie anointed his hands with oil, touched Quinton, and began to pray. Then Q said, "Oh, I remember!" Evidently, some raccoons had crossed the road in his pathway. In trying to avoid hitting them, he lost control of the car. His Uncle Maurice (Elbert's father) told him, "Next time, bust 'em, man!" We all laughed. I was glad to have Q on the mend. I am so glad that God allowed my son and nephew to live. I believe in predestination and divine purpose. The prayer helped him mend speedily. Why shouldn't I praise continually?

Another testimony concerns one of the girls. In April 2006, my youngest daughter, my namesake, Bonney, was in the hospital from Monday evening until Friday afternoon. Never would I have imagined that I would be in the hospital with a sick child on this wise. Even with nine children, hospital visits and stays were not a normal, frequent occurrence for our family. As I said earlier, we are blessed. The doctors did not seem to be able to come up with a definite diagnosis of her condition. Test after test came back negative. Then, just a few months later, this same child was in a head-on collision.

As I look back, now I see that the sickness or the collision could have been unto death. We prayed. We had others to pray and God delivered her. Grace and mercy covered my child. God above had tender mercy on us so that we would not bear that loss. I know it is because He has predestined purpose for her life.

My praise to God will know no end. I want to share what I have kept in mind through the years when life was difficult. These affirmations of praise brought me through every time:

- I'm saved … Thank you, Lord.
- I have a wonderful, saved husband … Thank you, Lord.

- We understand the importance of relationship -vs. -religion … Thank you, Lord.
- We have children and, grandchildren … Thank you, Lord.
- We have extended families, neighbors, and friends … Thank you, Lord.
- We have our home, land, vehicles, etc. … Thank you, Lord.
- We have received recognition in magazines and newspapers … Thank you, Lord.
- The family has been blessed with musical talent, scholastic excellence, financial endowments, great jobs, opportunities, overseas travel, enrichment enhancements, skills, abilities, knowledge, and understanding … Thank you, Lord.
- We have gone through tests, trials, tribulations, conflict, confrontations, and times of laughter, times of tears, winter, spring, summer, and fall … Thank you, Lord.
- I will bless the Lord at all times! His praise shall continually be in my mouth.

To end this section, I want to share a testimony where there was pronounced divine intervention. It happened on April 11, 2012.

> I have to take a praise break right now. It is 11:22 p.m., and I owe God praise. As I traveled back from Norfolk, Virginia, I was more tired and sleepy than I knew. All I remember is both hands on the wheel and turning the car from the right back on the road toward the left. I turned so hard and so quick until one of my arms hit the horn. I saw the mailbox right there to the right of the car. Visually, it looked like there should have been an impact. I braced myself for the impact that was coming. I felt no impact. I knew then that God had sent an angel to protect me. A collision that should have occurred, miraculously, God blocked it. I made it home safely. His faithfulness, love, intervention and continual answers to prayer, fuel my praise to God.

With a grateful heart, I offered this prayer: "God, I thank You for the angels You dispatched to watch over me tonight. Lord, You took me to my destination safely and brought me back home safely. I thank You for protection. I believe there is still work for me to do. Help me, Lord, to do Your work and Your will. God, You blocked the accident on tonight, and I thank You. Hallelujah!!! Oh, bless the name of God!"

I thank God for the power of prayer.

CHAPTER 6

Understanding the Legacy of Love

My life may seem insignificant to many. However, my life holds intrigue and a measure of curiosity for those who do not know me personally and of my faith in God. So, people often ask how we made it, and how all the kids have managed to be successful to this day. What could I write to help someone else in response to these questions? Here are a few questions and my attempt to answer them.

FAQ'S (Frequently Asked Questions) ... Answers
Why does parenting get frustrating at times? I got a personal revelation. Sometimes, even in parenting, we have expectations of a return. Now I know why I'm feeling frustrated. I do what I do, thinking I will get good back. That is the wrong motive. I should do what is right because it is the right thing to do. Whether I get a returned favor, I must make sure my motives are pure. Being a good mom and doing good things for my children does not guarantee the children doing good things back to me. That was my revelation. Forgive me, Lord, for the wrong motives. Help me live holy for You, before my children, by being a good example. Without this revelation, it's possible to become frustrated. As parents, we provide care, food, provision, etc. for our children. They seem so ungrateful sometimes. As parents, whether they are

ungrateful or grateful, we should do what we do because it's the right thing to do.

The curiosity factor may include such questions as, ***Just how did you stay married for 39 years?*** We are still together for 39 years by the grace of God. There are so many things that we have gone through that could have broken our marriage into pieces. Having good role models has been a great help. When you are able to see a couple that has been successful, it helps. Connie and Shirley Sawyer have been great role models. They weathered many tests and trials, yet maintained a strong, loving, God-centered marriage for 62 years. God in the marriage makes for a successful marriage. Even though Pop Sawyer has gone on to receive his reward, he left a clear picture of what a godly husband, father, grandfather, brother, uncle, and friend looks like. He was indeed a great man of love, faith and integrity.

Of course, communication is important. Listening and hearing your spouse is critical. Loving each other through all situations is foundational. It is important to accept and love your spouse for who they are. It is not fair to try to change them into who they are not. For example, if you would ask my husband, "What is Bonnie's favorite color?" He would answer, "Red." If you would ask him my favorite animal, he would say, "Her favorite animal is an elephant." He has taken the time to get to know me. He has taken the time to deem important the things that are important to me. Marriage is all about relationship, loving, caring, compromise, commitment, patience, sacrifice, selective amnesia, forgiveness, trust, and understanding. I Corinthians 13 gives an in-depth viewpoint on characteristics of love. If you want a happy, healthy marriage, consider this scripture. If you want a relationship that will flourish, consider this scripture. Allow me to share again a portion of this scripture, I Corinthians 13: 3–8, from The Message Bible.

So, no matter what I say, what I believe, and what I do, I'm bankrupt without love:

Love never gives up.

Love cares more for others than for self.

Love doesn't want what it doesn't have.

Love doesn't strut,

Doesn't have a swelled head,

Doesn't force itself on others,

Isn't always "me first,"

Doesn't fly off the handle,

Doesn't keep score of the sins of others,

Doesn't revel when others grovel,

Takes pleasure in the flowering of truth,

Puts up with ...,

Trusts God always,

Always looks for the best,

Never looks back,

But keeps going to the end.

Love never dies...

How were you able to provide a college education for them?
Once again, I must confess that God did it. I used to ponder and think about how all my children would receive further education. A college education can be extremely expensive. To give you the

bottom line, we tithed, gave liberal offerings, remained faithful to God, and trusted in God to take care of it all. Preparing for college did not begin in high school. Preparing for college begins on the first day of education. Actually, preparing began before they ever step foot into the classroom. Their first learning experience happened in the home. None of my children ever attended day care. (You do the math of how much that would have cost for nine children. I really do not know; I am guessing it would be thousands and thousands of dollars.) I was able to be home with them. What a blessing!

From day one, the children must have a respect and discipline concerning education. My children knew they were to learn at school. It was not okay for them to cause trouble, be disrespectful, fight, use bad language, demonstrate bad behavior, and not do their assigned work. Your name and reputation are important. The family is important, also. Reputation and family name matter in life. I know my children received correction and discipline many times because of their grandparents and parents. Moreover, I expected their response to be, "Yes, sir! No, sir! Yes, ma'am! No, ma'am!" If there was ever a problem, it was for parents and teachers to resolve.

No child of mine had the liberty to disrespect teachers, even if it seemed as if the teacher was being unfair or partial. My oldest set the standard high. Connie excelled in academics, was involved in athletics, active in our community, participated in church ministry, and was just well- rounded. I could say the same for all of our nine children. Everything affects everything else. What you begin in primary school carries over into middle school. In addition, appropriate mannerisms in middle school set you up for success in high school. High school is the final stepping-stone for a college education. Theoretically, one should not have to pay for education. There are grants and scholarships (academic/athletic) available. If you were to ask my children to share their individual experience, they could tell you in detail. They wrote the essays, asked for letters of recommendation, filled out applications, and honored deadlines.

We did not do for them the things that they needed to do for themselves.

When I tell you that we prayed, fasted, and trusted in God, you might say, "Great! But how did you educate all of your children?" My true response would be, "God did it!" Even as I typed those words, I need to share that time is of the essence. Timing is everything. It is always important to honor deadlines. Instill in your children that truth. We know that favor isn't fair. Nevertheless, we can't expect rules to bend just because we choose not to turn in paperwork at the appropriately assigned timeline. As we do what we must do, God steps in with His awesomeness and works it all out, and so He gets all the glory.

How important was the homework process? Early on, we made it imperative to our children that they be serious about their studies. What they have achieved, they achieved themselves. You do a disservice to your child to do their work for them. They wrote their own essays, did their own homework, and completed their own projects. Do you get the picture? It is pure insanity to expect a kindergartner to produce work equal to what an adult would produce. Can I be honest? New math ... old math ... At one point in time, I helped the children with math to the best of my ability.

I used knowledge from when I was in school. The next day, my child came home from school and said, "Ma, what you told me was wrong. We have to do it a different way!" We may have gotten the same answer, but the process was different. I learned early on about peer tutoring. I quickly learned how to send the younger ones to the older ones for help. When they asked me the meaning of words or how to spell the words, I did not always just give the answer. Many times, they had to go through the process of looking the words up in the dictionary. You cripple your child if you do their work for them. For instance, if the child doesn't understand first-grade work, they will have no foundation to build upon for second-grade work.

Don't take the struggle away from your child. What they work for in education will remain with them for a lifetime. Reading is fundamental. Correct when necessary, but praise them often.

Encouragement goes a long way. Make a big deal out of their great accomplishments.

What was family life like when the children were younger?
When the children were younger, family life was a challenge. Warning: live within the budget of what you can afford. I made the mistake of trying to go way outside of what I could afford at Christmas time to get what I wanted for the children. I know now that was not smart. I would be months into the next year trying to recoup. Please don't make my same mistake.

Sharing was just a normal part of everyday living. If you were going to use your siblings' clothing, respect them and ask. We passed clothes down from oldest to youngest. Clothes got altered and mended. It was not always easy to pass shoes down. The clothes that were worn and torn and everything in between became 'play clothes.' When you came in from school, you had to change out of your best clothes into your 'play clothes.' This was done so that your best clothes would last longer.

I tried to instill in my children to be happy with what they had. I wanted them to know that they are more than the clothes they wore and the shoes on their feet. I could not afford name brand clothes unless they were on sale. However, I would keep their clothes clean and mended. I was not an advocate of them borrowing clothes from family or friends.

If you can't afford something, why borrow it? If you borrow something and you damage it, then you have to replace what you really cannot afford. That just does not make sense to me. It is as if you covet what somebody else has. Be happy with who you are and what you have. ·

A dear friend, Ma Dessie, gave CC a bunk bed that needed just a little work. What a treasure! CC took that bunk bed as a pattern and made three more sets. For nine children, we then had eight beds. My two youngest sons had to share a bed. I really felt blessed that at least we were able to provide that luxury. Before the bunk beds, it was three or four children to one bed. At one point in time, the bed my three oldest slept on was a pull-out sofa bed. The sofa bed was a gift from my father.

Always, we tried to teach them to be thankful for what was prepared to eat and not be wasteful. It was not cool to waste food or complain about the food placed before you. I respect people who just cannot stomach certain foods. In fact, as a baby, CC had to drink goat's milk. Even now, he does not like milk or mayonnaise. However, his parents taught him not to waste food. As a young boy in school, he drank his milk real fast (a hard task) and then ate his food. Eventually, he stopped getting milk altogether, or he shared it with others.

In fact, some children declare they don't like a certain food. They come to this conclusion without even tasting it. Sometimes they just don't like the way it looks or smells. Many times, once they taste the food, they actually like it. We would not force them to eat something if it made them physically sick. If I prepared a meal and they did not like all of the entrees, they would eat what they could and be thankful. I did not prepare another complete meal just to satisfy their taste buds.

Did you have it all in the early years of marriage? No! No! No! What held us together was love. We still do not have it all. However, I believe we are rich in what really matters. We love and care about one another. We share what we have. We enjoy spending time together. We are a family of love. We pray for one another. We celebrate with each other. We encourage each other. We share in the victories and in the struggles.

I can tell you for a surety that our God is a provider. We tithe and give an offering, and God is mighty in honoring His Word and providing every need. Even when I have made bad decisions financially, God still did not forsake us. Through the tests and trials, we learned, and our faith strengthened. We do know God as an on-time God. He may not come when we want (learned patience), but He is on time (expressed gratitude).

Where does God, faith, family, and unity fit into the big picture of your life story? Our faith in God has always been the foundation upon which we built our family. We have all experienced the power of God working. Our faith strengthens daily. Think about it! If there is no test, there can be no testimony!

Our children had no choice about attending church. We attended church as a family. The conversation was more like, "Hurry up and get ready so we won't be late for church!" The response was, "Yes, sir! Yes, ma'am!"

We are a unified family. However, that does not mean that we always see things eye -to -eye. We have our disagreements and opinions. After all is said and done, we are still family, and we love each other. We understand that it would be foolish to let anything or anyone come between the family bonds. When I talk about a family member, am I not doing damage to myself? Nor should I allow anyone to run down my family. It does get personal. The family should be one, unified. Where there is unity, there is strength.

> "Behold, how good and how pleasant it is for
> brethren to dwell together in unity!"
> Psalm 133:1
> "And if a house be divided against itself, that
> house cannot stand." Mark 3:25
> "Most important of all, continue to show deep love for each
> other, for love covers a multitude of sins." I Peter 4:8

How did you feed such a large family? What was your grocery bill like? The Lord, true to His Word, provided for us. "But my God shall supply all your need according to his riches in glory by Christ Jesus." Philippians 4:19 Providing took effort. At one point in time, we had chickens. They provided fresh brown eggs and eventually meat. Success with hunting provided some meat. For many years, CC would hunt for deer, rabbit, squirrel, and raccoon. Sometimes, we took the deer meat to a local store and they made sausage for us. Fishing was not for sport. Fishing provided food in the freezer for future meals. I have been fishing, cleaned the fish, packed them in a Ziploc bag, and filled the bag with water to keep them fresh. This girl from Chesapeake suburbia really lived life in a different manner. This road down memory lane reminds me of the hog killings we used to have. The hog killings were great, messy, and smelly! I helped clean the chitterlings.

In addition, CC planted a garden. He planted greens, collards, tomatoes, string beans, butter beans, okra, cucumbers, peppers, squash, zucchini, snow peas, corn, field peas, onions, and I hope I have not forgotten anything. Thus, we had fresh vegetables. We often had enough produce to share with family and friends. In addition, we have a fig bush and a grape vine that have produced abundantly through the years. Ma taught me how to can and freeze fruits and vegetables. I learned how to make fig preserves, jams, and jellies. In the fields, I gleaned potatoes, cabbage, and broccoli. I have been to pick strawberries and grapes. Even though I had to pay for my strawberries and grapes, overall, we ate very well.

Of course, we purchased staples such as… flour, sugar, seasonings, milk, eggs, meat, etc. The grocery bill was really not that bad. I learned from my mom, as well as Ma, how to make a little bit stretch. I've seen my mom (Mamie) go in the store with $20 and shop for the family. If she had to put something back during the check-out process because she did not have enough money to cover it all, that is what happened. I learned from Ma (Shirley) that the grocery bill was a place that I could save, put that money to the side, and save up for emergencies.

I learned how to make homemade biscuits, rolls, fried okra, molasses pudding, pickles, Irish potatoes, squash, sweet potato pie, apple pie, … etc. I learned how to take one chicken or a little bit of meat, cut it up, make some gravy, accompany it with some vegetables, rice, biscuits, homemade fig preserves, and feed the entire family. It was actually a feast. I really did not know how to cook that well before I got married. Warning: Moms, bring your daughters in the kitchen with you and teach them all that you know. If you don't, you will be doing them a disservice. Even now, if there is something about cooking that I am not sure about, I will ask Ma. She knows.

How expensive was it to clothe such a large family? First, allow me to say, 'thank you!' I owe a debt of gratitude to family members and friends, known/anonymous, for giving me clothes for my children. The expense was as much or as little as I chose to make it. After receiving so many gifts of clothing for my children, I became spoiled.

After many years of blessings, when it was time to go buy clothes, I was shocked at the price of clothes. Trust me. It did not take long for me to realize that there was no need for me to try to keep up with the 'Joneses.' Children outgrow clothes and shoes so fast. Many times, normal wear and tear will shorten the life of a pair of shoes or clothes. A mandate to have name brand clothes and high-priced, expensive shoes was not on my agenda. What was important to me was to use the gifts of clothes, purchase what I could afford, and keep them clean, ironed, pressed, neat, and presentable. It was hilarious to me when people would hesitate to bless me. They were actually afraid that I would reject my blessing. The conversation would go something like this, "I have some things that maybe your children could use. Would you like to have them? I don't mean to offend you and …"Probably, before they could finish rattling on, I would say, "Yes, yes, yes! Thank you so much!"

Some angels in my life waited until I left home and blessed me while I was gone. It was like Christmas. When I returned home, I found bags and bags of clothes on the porch, waiting for me to sort through. What a mighty God we serve. I must inform you that my blessings included very nice things. Not just play clothes, school clothes, and church clothes; but also clothes I could put aside until the children reached that particular size. I guess you could say I had now and later clothes. At one point in time, my cup was running over.

I had so many bags of clothes stored in the upstairs attic until I had to sort through them. Amazingly, I was able to be a blessing to others. I often told my children that if you have a closed fist, sure, nothing gets out but nothing can enter. If your hand is open, there can be a flow. When it was time to sort through their wardrobes, I excitedly told them, "Make room for your blessings!" God always provided for our needs like clothes, undergarments, socks, tights, shoes, hats, boots, coats, jackets, gloves… everything.

My mom taught me how to sew. I also took home economics in school. So, I used to sew Easter dresses, suits, shorts, skirts, jumpers, quilts, jammers, handkerchiefs, vests, bow ties, robes, and neckties. (I even ordered labels for and sold ties. Some of my handmade ties have been given as gifts around the world … Uganda, South Korea) Because of their humble upbringing, my children, know what it means to dare to be different.

There is certainly more I could say, but these are my answers to frequently asked questions. If you have questions for me, feel free to reach out to me on my blog: https://blessed2bbndsawyer.wordpress.com. It would be my pleasure to correspond with you.

In the next chapters of this book, enjoy what the children have to share. They are carriers of the legacy of love. God had a destiny for them through the things we all went through together. It is our prayer that as you read their sections, you will see the fruit of all that I have shared in this book.

CHAPTER 7

Reflections from the Legacy Bearers

Y ou have read about many life events of my family. Now, in the next chapters, we want to get insight from the recipients and future promoters of the legacy of love. In this chapter, we will get reflections from the oldest three children and their spouses. I call them the legacy bearers because chief responsibility always falls on the oldest siblings.

Connie W. Sawyer III

Apologies up front if Josh has already written (or will write) something similar, but this had to be said. I have a ton for which to thank my dad and mom. Along with being the primary shapers and reinforcers of my earlier spiritual life and a continual source of inspiration and guidance today, they both contributed in a special way to forming desires in me for certain activities. I could go on and on about how my dad taught me how to love sports, even when I was not (and still am not) very good at any one. However, I'm grateful to my mom and her planting a love of music in my siblings and me, especially since it's become so much of a part of who we are.

As I prepare now for another Sunday morning of service at my church, I think on how the members of my church— choir members, congregants, other musicians— often comment about the joy they see in my service. I'll be the first to admit, I'm not the best musician in the world. Sure, I've played the saxophone for almost 24 years now. I've been blessed to have many opportunities to learn, to share, and to grow in this skill; but, I'm humbled when people are able to see how much fun I'm having when I play. There's a good reason for that.

For as long as I can remember, there's been a piano at the house. I can't remember how the first one got there, but I remember our eventually having the very piano that took residence in my grandparents' home. True, it was sometimes a bit out of tune, and it was sometimes a battle to share with others in the family; but it was the foundation of many of us learning to love music. We weren't always permitted to listen to secular music, and were often limited in what we could access, but we were able to learn. Mom was a great teacher, though there were times when her lessons were a chore. I managed to have her at my services for two years, and for some unbeknownst reason, I thought that was plenty. Little did I know that seeds were being planted for what I am today.

Right before my tenth birthday, my school presented the opportunity for us to join a band. After hearing the exploits of my uncles on both sides of the family, I wanted nothing more than to play an instrument. For some reason, the saxophone just screamed out to me. So, I had to make a huge sell to my parents to spend the $835 dollars to buy a new instrument. I'm so glad they didn't push me to a cheaper instrument.

Over time, people were impressed with how quickly I took to this music thing. I was able to relate notes on my horn to notes in concert pitch, and I was hungry to practice as much as I could. My practice methods were unconventional, but normally involved a few minutes of scales, with a few minutes of practicing to whatever songs (to which we could listen) played on the radio. I think most of where

I am today has to do with my piano-playing background (as limited as it was) and an ability to actually play what I hear; and, of course, the patience of my parents to let me use this method. It led to two memories that have shaped my posture as a musician even today.

I remember the first time I played in the church. My uncles told me that I couldn't play until I had completed my first "semester" in the band at school. Undaunted, I kept practicing until that time, and I got to play with the children's choir. I was nervous, I was anxious, and I really didn't have an idea what I would do. All I could do was close my eyes and do what I could. After a while, everything was done. It seemed that it was a blessing, and I kept playing there until I left for college. Looking back now, the funny part about this memory is not the reaction of the congregation, but more than that, the emotions that I experienced. Anytime I am asked to play now, this seems to be how things go. I get nervous, I get anxious, I don't know what I'll do, I close my eyes and I just play. I don't know why, but that's my comfort zone; I guess that's when I'm in my element.

The other story began before my freshman year in college. Band in high school wasn't really the coolest thing to do, but it kept me with some sort of instruction to go along with my playing in the church. And when preparing to attend college, I realized right away the need for me to continue some sort of formal involvement. That's why I decided, of course, to try out for the marching band. After nine years in the band, including five years in marching band and three years as drum major, I figured this was an easy thing. I remember the assistant director at the time looking at me afterward and holding in laughter. He and I knew that it wasn't my day. I was more than comfortable being an alternate and finding another way to keep my dream alive. Thank God, it went a little differently.

A couple of weeks before school started, my dad called me while I was out. The assistant director had now become the director of bands and was calling to see if I was still interested in marching. Needless to say, I was in Chapel Hill in a week. So much happened as a result of this incident – I found a community of great friends I have until this day. My involvement in the marching band hopefully, encouraged six younger siblings to march in the same band, and the Fuchs family now has a special place in the hearts of all the Sawyer family. Not to mention I managed to end up in a formation within the first week of band camp with a special young lady. She may have thought I was small, skinny, and loud back then; but something changed over time. Now, eighteen years later, we're husband and wife.

I think that explains my joy in playing my sax. There's a certain peace that comes with doing what you know you should be doing. Not to mention the joy in knowing that you're right where you need to be at the right time. It may not manifest itself at that time, and it may not even manifest itself in the same way it did for me. However, when you're doing what God has gifted you to do, and when you know that you're giving your all to do His will, there should be a corresponding joy that the world cannot help but notice. So Yes, I smile, have fun, and enjoy every time I get the opportunity to play. I think about all the things I've encountered through my life (sickness, injury, rejection, etc.) that momentarily got in the way of my using this gift. Then I think that those things did not permanently silence me. Sometimes, my laughter and my smiling is just my way of showing the world how blessed I feel to be given the opportunity to serve in my little way.

So, yeah, thanks Mom for forcing those piano lessons on me. Those were two of the best years I've ever spent. I hope the joy I've brought to so many people, and the blessing that I endeavor to be for the Kingdom, are enough to pay back that $835. Even my wife has been a partaker of your legacy of love.

Alicia Johnson Sawyer

I can remember the very first time I saw him. It was a hot summer day in 1996, a few days into the marching band camp at the University of North Carolina at Chapel Hill. He was wearing a white t-shirt, black shorts, a straw hat, and black-rimmed glasses. He had a saxophone strapped around his neck, and he was crossing over a ditch. That was the very first time I remember seeing Connie W. Sawyer, III. He'll tell you the first time he saw me was earlier that spring when he was on campus interviewing for scholarships. I played the flute during the dinner reception of one of his scholarship interview weekends. Though I remember playing the flute at the reception, I don't remember meeting him. I've asked him before if he was touched by my brilliant and moving flute performance that evening such that he remembered me playing, even though we weren't introduced. He just said I did "all right"!

By being in the marching band together, we became friends, but it wasn't until a Tuesday evening in February of 1998 that I thought that this could develop into something more. He offered to walk me back to my dorm room after a music rehearsal. I can't remember now what we talked about, but I do remember being impressed with his intelligence and the fact that he could offer thoughtful discussion about such a wide variety of topics. A topic I do remember talking about was the stars. He talked about how clear the sky was, how bright the stars were when he was camping outside in an Outward Bound experience, how that experience changed him and made him appreciate God, his family, and his life.

We dated … throughout the rest of college…throughout a summer of him going to Colorado… throughout him going to South Africa for a summer and doing a self-guided tour, where he played his saxophone in various cities in South Africa… throughout a summer of him going to the Dominican Republic and leading other young people on a health mission … through him coming back early from the Dominican Republic because he got sick. I have a huge stack of the printouts of the e-mails and letters we exchanged during those times. They bring a smile to my face to read the many recaps of our days, how we were missing each other. I also never realized how cheesy I was (OK, I still am) until I pull out those letters, but they are a treasure, and I'll never get rid of them.

After graduating in 1999, I stayed behind at Carolina to do some post-graduate work, while Connie completed his undergraduate studies. In 2000, after he graduated, Connie traveled to what he now refers to as just "the City." He went off to law school at Columbia University in New York, New York. For a year, we corresponded, e-mailed, and called. I caught plane tickets to New York whenever I could. In 2001, I packed up my bags and followed him up to New York to work as a legal assistant for a law firm located at Four Times Square. It was a different life, in so many ways. I got an apartment in Flushing in Queens and had to ride the #7 Subway all the way into Times Square to my job. Connie stayed in Morningside Heights, first on 110th and later on 112th Streets in Manhattan. His first place was the size of a closet. You could turn on the TV, open the window, get something from the fridge, and open the door while still touching the bed!

The two of us, small-town North Carolina kids, were in New York when 9-11 occurred. I think he was the first person I called when I was at my desk on my job listening to the news reports and trying to figure out what to do. He was the person I was looking for when I had to walk over 70 blocks later the morning of September 11, when everybody was trying to evacuate any high-profile skyscraper in Manhattan. He was the person I called when, in the following days, the building had reports of bomb threats, and we had to evacuate multiple times. There's a lot about New York that is good and vibrant, and Connie's experience of New York was substantially different and more positive than mine. I will say that there's a spot on Broadway near 112th Street that will always have a fond memory in my heart. It was the place where Connie proposed to me on August 23, 2002.

Connie got a job in Charlotte, North Carolina, in the office of a large international law firm, and we returned to North Carolina after he graduated from law school in 2003. We got married on August 23, 2003, exactly a year after we became engaged. A lot has happened since then. From a professional standpoint, after working as a banking and finance attorney for several years, Connie has now begun his solo law practice and is much happier now. I started working at a Charlotte law firm in 2004, first as a legal secretary, and more recently as a paralegal in the commercial real estate practice.

From a family standpoint, after two years of infertility and then two miscarriages, God blessed us with a beautiful baby girl. Lauryn Caroline was born on March 27, 2008, and is simply a joy! She's so full of personality and humor, and compassion. I think the best of both Connie and me is wrapped up in this little girl. I think she's inherited her daddy's musicality, and I truly hope she's got his sense of direction. She loves to sing and dance and get her nails painted, and she loves soccer (at least today she does). We tried t-ball, and though she was excited about the fashion because what girl, after all, doesn't love a hat color coordinated with an outfit. She enjoys soccer a tad more. She also recently had her "theater debut" as Suzy Snowflake in her school's Christmas play this past winter. In my completely unbiased opinion, she made the whole show. From a musical standpoint, Connie continues to use his gift. I can't forget music; because, after all, Connie and I met at a band camp! He is truly and unequivocally anointed by God to play his saxophone. He plays for our church and in a group named Groove Masters. Groove Masters was founded by another church musician. Also, Groove Masters won the Charlotte Music Awards' Best Jazz Band Award in 2009 and continue to play in various venues and functions in the greater Charlotte area. I still pick up my flute from time to time and play a Carolina fight song or two, but that's about it these days unless someone can give me some sheet music and a month to practice. I wonder if Lauryn will choose the flute as one of her instruments of choice, but if she chooses the saxophone, that'll be fine, too.

After more than 14 years of being together and almost 8 years of marriage, Connie and I have been through a lot. We've had very good times, and we've had times when one of us has almost had to scrap the other off the floor. But then again, we are a testimony to the Bible verse that says that two are better than one. One of us has been strong when the other has needed help. I admire, respect, and love Connie for so many things. He's a God-fearing man, strong yet sensitive, smart, compassionate, generous, a hard worker, a fabulous husband, and a great father. There have been many times when we're sitting in the living room watching a sport of some kind or another when I say to him, "I love you and thank you for choosing me to be your wife." He'll ask, "What did I do?" And I'll respond, "It's not what you did. It's who you are." He probably still thinks I'm cheesy. OK, he says to strike "probably." He does think

I'm cheesy, but I don't care. I'm just speaking the truth. The best part is that God willing, there's still a lot of our story left to live.

2016 Update

Thank God, we have, indeed, been living more of our story. The addition of our son, Connie W. Sawyer, IV ("Wil") in 2013 has added even more blessings, noise, and laughter to our family. He is a bundle of kinetic energy, talkative, playful, active, friendly, a connoisseur of any and all athletic balls that can be bounced, kicked, dribbled or thrown (and, for that matter, anything that *resembles* an athletic ball; many an orange and an apple have met a sad fate before they could be sliced and eaten). He has earned his nickname of Boom in several ways: (i) as the fourth generation Connie, we sometimes called him C-4 as an infant (C-4 is used in explosives), (ii) as an infant he was loud...as a toddler he was louder, and most recently ..., (iii) he loves music generally and particularly, he loves the drums. His godfather gave him a drum set several months ago and since then he has banged on those drums daily...and loudly. BOOM!

Few things are as sweet as the sound of Lauryn's and Wil's laughter blending together as they play together. I hear Lauryn teaching her brother the alphabet or helping him to wash his hands and I'm startled at how quickly the time has flown. It seems just like yesterday I was running over the same things with her. Wil adores his big sister and follows her like a shadow, sometimes to her frustration but usually to her delight.

For Connie, of course, sibling relationships are an old hat. Having grown up an only child, I'm still learning how to adjudicate wisely over serious matters like the stubborn refusal to share a toy or what to do when our two-year-old son hits our seven-year-old daughter and she reciprocates in kind. All of us are learning and growing in our different and individual ways and, importantly, we are learning and growing together as a family. Lauryn, once my little Suzie Snowflake, still loves to dance. She also loves to draw and paint and do crafts. She has an imagination second to none and has even developed a set of blueprints for a family development center that she wants to build one day - complete with children-oriented fun zones, a parent zone and a list of rules and procedures that must be followed for everyone's safety.

She is so like me. She is so Connie. She is so much her own person and it is truly my honor and pleasure to parent her. Connie, as the head of our household, does an awesome job of articulating and embodying the values that we believe and practice. The four of us were recently riding in the car and passed by another car that was boldly flying a big Confederate flag from its tailgate. I think I just said "wow" when we saw it, but Lauryn heard me and asked why I had reacted in the way I did. Connie, as only he can, was able to explain to our young children why that flag is such a charged symbol to us and the complicated legacy of the Civil War. Importantly, he didn't just leave it there. He reminded the children that despite how we may view that symbol, as children of God, we are to love and to show love to everybody, even people who do things that we don't agree with. That's the kind of man he is. That's the kind of people we strive to be.

Before we leave the house in the mornings, the four of us gather together and grasp hands, readying ourselves to pray together. We close our eyes and bow our heads. Lauryn's quiet voice breaks the silence as she prays for Connie and me and Wil...for our health and our safety, as she thanks God for a brand-new day and new opportunities. At the moment just after we say amen, at the moment when we are leaning in for a group hug, just as we are saying "I love you" to each other before we go out into our places in the world, at that moment when we are all connected to each other and to God, I think, this is what it's all about.

Joshua Dan Sawyer

"Are you finished?" I can remember growing up when my mom and dad would have these long conversations with us, usually over something we did or, over a poor decision we made. I can distinctly recall standing by the dresser in their bedroom, looking at my feet while they spoke to me, and thinking to myself, "Are you finished?" (though I would never say that out loud). Even though I was the one in the wrong, I wanted for them to end the discussion so that I would not have to keep dealing with the consequences, but so that I could also begin the path to making changes.

Life has a way of doing the same thing to us. We are given dreams, visions, passions, and desires. However, somewhere along the way, we make certain decisions, and some of those dreams are postponed. Many go through life never seeming to accomplish anything. Even worse are those who start a lot of things, but never seem to complete anything. To those who feel frustrated with your life situation, I will ask the same question that I asked (in my head) my parents, and that I've often asked myself; the same question that life often asks us, "Are you finished?"

I Corinthians 15:58 says, "Therefore, my beloved brethren, be ye stedfast, unmoveable, always abounding in the work of the Lord, forasmuch as ye know that your labour is not in vain in the Lord."

When it's all said and done, when this life as we know it is over with, please don't be left singing the "coulda-shoulda-woulda" song, because by then it's too late. Make sure you do all with this life that you have been called to do. God has given you all you need in order to do what He has called you to do, and He has also provided you with what you need to be successful (Deut. 8:18). Don't just be the type of person who can get the job. Be the person who can get the job done.

I can always remember counting games with my eight brothers and sisters. There was the consistent 1-20, and when playing hide-and-go-seek, there was the "5, 10, 15, 20." (At this point, we always break in song). However, when trying to decide who had the most, we always tried to outdo each other. "I have 10! … I have 100!… I have 1,000!…" At this point, I thought I was doing something, so I said, "I have infinity!" Thinking I had this thing locked down, my older brother, Connie, would come back with, "I have infinity plus one!"

At this point, I'm crushed. However, next time, I had his number. Once I got hit with the "plus one, 1", I came back with "Infinity plus infinity!" I had him this time; but of course, with him never being one to get beat (even to this day), he came back with "Infinity times infinity!" As I said, I couldn't win.

Mathematically, we know that infinite represents a concept of a number which is larger than any number you can imagine. So, if you think about the largest number possible, you can always "add 1" or "multiply it times itself." It's amazing that numbers never end, and even more amazing that, as you study this concept of an unreachable number, there are actually many consistencies. We can use infinite to study end behaviors, limits, and, in some cases, find values of convergent series. I discovered two main points as this relates to life. There is always more (1) in you, and (2) for you.

1. **There's always more in you.** Many times, we feel that we have given everything we have into our commitments. We feel that our jobs, spouses, children, churches, family members, friends, bills, worries, stresses, illnesses, debts, struggles, and cares of this life have taken everything we have. We feel that our strength is gone and that our hope, our dreams, and our motivation are gone. We have to remember that there is always more in us. There is always more strength for us to carry out the tasks we have been called to do. Paul states in II Corinthians 4:16 (KJV), "For which cause we faint not; but though our outward man perish, yet the inward man is renewed day by day."

2. **There's always more for you.** The general nature of the average person is to accept what they have as what will always be. Disappointments often cause us to feel that what we have is all we will ever have. Successes cause us to feel that what we have accomplished is enough for our lives. I would like to dispel both of these myths, and encourage you that there is always more for you. There is more to be gained in this life, through faith in Jesus Christ, and through deliberate and, focused actions toward carefully planned goals. Remember, we serve a God who can do "exceeding, abundantly above all that we can ask or think" (Ephesians. 3:20, KJV). Also, for those who have

"arrived," there is still work to be done. If you are still here, you still have a chance to accomplish more, or to share your successes with others, and create a legacy of success. Remember, "We must work while it is day…" (John 9:4).

Don't throw in the towel. Hang in there, and finish the job you were destined to do. Become who you were destined to be. There's always more!!! Class dismissed.

Sh'Rhonda Jones Sawyer
You There?
Posted on August 3, 2013
https://yepbuddy.wordpress.com/
Joshua Sawyer 5M: Math, Music, Marriage, Money, Manhood

I love hearing my wife's voice. Period. So, sometimes, for no reason, I will call her while she's at work, or while she's away. I really don't want to talk about anything in particular, I just want to hear her smile. Now, depending on where I am, or what's going on around me, sometimes it's hard to hear what she is saying. In order for us to fully understand each other, there has to be a clear line of communication. In order to make sure I can hear her heart, I sometimes ask the question, "you there?" To be successful, we must ask the same question. We must decide if we are in a place where we can receive vision and walk into our destiny.

The first reason I find that I have to ask this question is because we have a poor connection. Signal reception can be decreased due to poor weather, thick walls on buildings, or being in places where service is not normally provided. Life is that way at times. Storms, tests, and trials make it hard to hear God clearly. Past hurts and pains cause us to shut ourselves in, and shut Him out. Sometimes we are in places where only a few people are shining their light. In either case, we must not forget He is there. For He (Jesus) hath said, "I will never leave thee, nor forsake thee." (Heb. 13:5). If there is a poor connection, it's on our end. We must then make sure we clear the line. Somehow, we must find a way to press through the clutter, and hear His direction for our lives. Psalms 37:23 teaches us that "The steps of a good man are ordered by the LORD: and he delighteth in his way". It goes on to tell us that even if that man makes a mistake, God will not cause it to be his demise.

To be successful, to achieve what God has purposed for your life, you must be there, on the line, waiting to hear from Him. Make sure you have a good, clear connection with God. Make sure He knows you. Make sure you are in a place where you can hear from Him. Don't be so busy, or preoccupied, that you fail to answer His call. If you are not where you want to be, first be THERE to hear from God. It's a pleasure to hear His heart, and His smile.

Quinton "Q" Leroy Sawyer

Surprise, I think, is the best way to describe the reaction I receive from people when they find out that I'm the third oldest child of nine to my parents. I would say that shock usually ensues when they find out that we all have the same mother and father, and that they are happily married still. Obviously, this is a bit of a rarity in this day and age. But then again, it is all I know, and I wouldn't have it any other way.

One of the cornerstones of my upbringing has been faith in God. Being raised in the church, we were all taught the basic values of a Christian lifestyle, including obedience. Ephesians 6:1 is a verse that has been stressed very early on, so when my mother sent the decree to her children that she required our assistance for her book, it was done. No questions asked. And I think that the best way for me to share my thoughts on my family is just to take a trip down memory lane.

The fondest memories of my life include my family. From reunions, Christmas gatherings, and graduation parties, to just casual gatherings at the house, we are definitely a family of love. I can remember my mom telling us that she used to walk around the house and count the heads of her children every night, just to make sure everyone was in their respective places as we slept. It usually wasn't too difficult to find us. The five boys shared two joining bedrooms, and the four girls all slept in the same room. I remember when Sister Boone gave my father a set of bunk beds. She was a family friend from our church in Norfolk, VA. Sis Boone had raised a fairly large family of her own, and after her children had grown and left the nest, she had little need for the bunk beds anymore.

My father, being the handyman that he always has been, took the bunk beds apart on Saturday morning. He measured them, each board, marked them, and took notes. Then, he took a trip to Lowe's in his truck and came back with lumber. That day, we replicated those bunk beds three times over. This was one of my lessons in taking something I had and making it stretch. Taking something and using it to get what I need, by just using a little brain power and elbow grease.

Growing up with that many people in such a confined space, we always bumped heads. By bumped heads I mean fought. By fought I mean closed fist, anywhere but the face and privates, brawls. My parents definitely did not condone nor allow this. Still, it happened. I think that, out of these experiences, a lot occurred. We definitely were tough kids. We had a fearful appreciation and respect for physical confrontations. However, most of all, we protected each other. Yeah, we may fight behind closed doors, but there was no way we allowed anyone outside the family to prey on any of us.

I can remember when Josh got into a fight during a summer 4-H camp day. I was told that after a quick flurry of one or two punches thrown, and no real injuries by either fighter, counselors broke up the fight. It was then that this guy proclaims to Josh that he'd be at our house to finish what he started, or something to that respect. Well, I wasn't present for the fight. Neither was Connie. However, we sure were standing right beside Josh, right in the entrance of the driveway, when this alleged 'bully' was to show. And we waited, but he never showed. I think that sense of duty has continued through our adult lives. We have done whatever we could to help each other, and protect each other from pain and harm, as best we could. Whether it was a place to crash, a few dollars, or even just an ear to lend, we've always been standing beside each other.

I definitely was a little kid who believed my parents could do anything in the world. Seriously, I literally believed my parents could do anything. I think I had good reason to believe so. My father wore suits to work, and traveled all over the country on business. However, when he got home, he always changed clothes and fixed everything. He was a plumber, electrician, auto mechanic, and carpenter. He hunted, fished, was a volunteer fireman, star on the softball field, and player in the old man recreational basketball pickup games. I literally thought he knew how to do everything in the world. My mother was just as amazing.

Being a homemaker with nine children, she did it all. Aside from the cooking, cleaning, hemming, crocheting, and other normal chores associated with raising children, my mom had her own business ventures. She made and even patented several reed basket designs for Watermark Association of Artisans. She taught piano lessons to beginners from the piano in our home. After Raymond began kindergarten, she finished her degree in Fine Arts and Music. She became very involved in the arts in the community, helping with the choir at the middle school, high school, and community college and teaching an interpretive dance to children in the local community. My parents definitely displayed a well-rounded lifestyle and encouraged all of their children to find their own interests and pursue them.

Another story, that I think shows a lot about me becoming the man I am today, occurred when I was a little boy. My dad was a country boy, and an avid hunter. We always had beagles for rabbit hunting, and early Saturday mornings in the fall were designed for rabbit hunting. I would always wake up when I could hear him leave the house. I'd rush to get my boots on, and my coat, and hurry outside to help him load the dogs into the truck for the hunting trip. After he went inside to kiss my mom goodbye, I'd ask if I could go with him. For many years, he'd tell me that I wasn't big enough yet, and I would sit on the front steps and cry while he drove away. I'm not sure that it was that I enjoyed hunting or it was just that I wanted to be like my dad, and I wanted to do the things he did. I think it's a great thing, too, that I had such a great example of a man to model myself after. I think I am the way I am today because of that example.

My parents required a lot of us during our childhood that we didn't necessarily enjoy or want. Sunday school was never an option. Piano lessons, 4-H club, sports teams, and Saturday Academy through ECSU Math and Science Education Network were things that we fought against but were required to be a part of anyway. It was through these endeavors that my parents were ensuring we would be well-rounded people. We were always required to be the best we could be in many different areas of life. Mentally, physically, and spiritually, we were required to grow and be the best we could be. Thus, we were also able to find our own interests, after exposure to so many different things. Even though I didn't enjoy those things while they were happening, I'm thankful for them now.

I think that one of the best things about my parents is their wisdom in dealing with me as their child. They seem to have developed an amazing ability to know what to say, when to say it, and how to say it in dealing with me. I think they have developed the awesome skill of being parents to adult children. My parents no longer tell me what to do (for the most part), but they understand that, as an adult, I have to make those decisions for myself. And rather than tell me what to do, they give their opinions on situations when I come to them with questions, give their best, Godly advice, then step back, and allow me to make my own decisions. I'm really thankful to have parents whose opinions I can listen to, trust, and use to make sound decisions. I understand that, in today's world, a lot of people my age don't have that luxury.

Needless to say, I'm very grateful for my family, my parents, and the things that I've gone through in my life. I know that, without a doubt, everything that my parents have done for me has been in an effort to keep me from unnecessary hurt or harm, and to help me grow up to be a responsible and productive citizen of this world. I thank them for the Christian values they've given to me, and the love they continue to show to me as an adult.

Lauren Coley Sawyer

May 30, 2015, will be a day that I will always remember. It was the day that I finally became a member of the Sawyer family and I became the wife of Quinton Leroy Sawyer, the family's third oldest child.

Quinton and I met October 2011 through mutual friends at a wedding in Washington, D.C., in which we served as a bridesmaid and groomsman. Our courtship was far from ordinary as it was long-distance for two years - I was living in Brooklyn, New York and Q had just moved to East Lansing, Michigan to work as an Athletic Trainer for the Michigan State University's Men's Basketball program. It was a whirlwind romance but we both knew where the relationship was going very early on. In the two months that I had known Q, we'd been on a first date, he met my mother and I had joined his *entire* family for their traditional Christmas Eve festivities.

Now let me be clear – I am an introvert. As the oldest of two children, I am quiet, thoughtful and value times of *peace*. When I first went to Camden for Christmas Eve, I was intimidated by the number of family members that were waiting for me and whether they would accept me, an unknown visitor, into their home and holiday traditions. But his brothers, sisters, in-laws and nieces and nephews all welcomed me with open arms. They embraced one another, laughed with one another and supported one another throughout the visit. It was something that I had not experienced growing up. My brother and I were not always on the best of terms. But this family, they were all best friends. Even better was the evidence of their faith that I witnessed that evening.

One of the reasons I fell for Q so quickly was due to his love for and the relationship he has built with his family members, especially his mother and father. I cherished and admire the respect he has for his parents. The way his face lights up when he talks about prior conversations with them or how they handled various childhood memories and milestones is one of my favorite things about him. Most of all, he knows the sacrifices that they made for their children over the years and respects them 100 percent. With this information, I knew they had successfully raised a God-fearing gentleman who, someday, would make a wonderful husband and father.

During the toasts on our wedding day, my father not only took the time to acknowledge Q and my journey together but he also took the opportunity to recognize Mr. Connie and Ms. Bonnie for raising nine successful and level-headed men and women. I'm so grateful to them for making Q the man he is today and am proud to be Lauren Coley Sawyer, continuing the legacy that they have started.

CHAPTER 8

Reflections from the Legacy Carriers

I n this chapter, we will continue to get reflections from the middle, three children. I call them the legacy carriers because they not only learned from my husband and me but from their older siblings. In addition, they had to teach the younger siblings as well. In this way, they are carriers of the legacy of love upward and downward in the family structure.

Portia Zaneta Sawyer Parker

You never realize how much strength you really have until you have to endure challenges in life. I can say that I am truly a strong person because of the example that I was given by my mother. I mean, who could be a ray of sunshine in a dark world? Mom. We always had a loving place to come home to after school, with a warm meal and a stern "no" if needed. She worked hard to keep us clean, rested, and happy. Of course, I didn't realize what she was instilling in me then, but it has made me into the strong person I am today. Being the oldest girl, I wanted to set an example for my sisters to be strong individuals, to go for your dreams, and be great at what you do in life. I remember them wanting to be with and around me, not knowing they appreciated my strength, even when I didn't see it in myself. I just did what I could to make it from day to day.

I decided after high school to attend the local university instead of the traditional school that my older brothers chose. That took strength. "Why?" You may ask. Because when you are different, you have to be strong enough to stand by your choices. I was able to experience college sports unlike any of my brothers or sisters. In college, I played volleyball and softball. Then again, being different requires being strong.

I know that life may not give us what we always want. We have to adjust and be strong through the ups and downs. I have three children whom I love dearly, and I realize now what my mom did for me growing up. She was strong for my well- being, and I want to do the same for my girls. They have given me the strength and inspiration to press forward, even when the situations around me say to give up. Philippians 4:13 is truly a scripture that has become well-known at "J-ma's" (my mom's) house. We have learned that we can do all things through Christ who gives us strength. Through everything I experience in life, I know that God will be my strength through it all. I can't take credit for making it this far; because it wasn't my doing but His. I am grateful for all the blessings God has given me and how He is allowing me to impact the lives of my daughters. I pray that they will grow up to be strong black women.

Crystal Denise Sawyer Chifunda – The "True" Middle Child

I get excited when I have the chance to talk to others about my family and tell of all the blessings and favors that God has bestowed upon us. I get energized and love it when I get to introduce people to my family because I am so proud of each and every one of them. Some people may call it bragging, and sometimes it may be, but I am not ashamed of my family, and I will tell the whole world about them.

As the true middle child, I like to think that I have my own unique view on what it means to be a part of this family. While six of my eight siblings can claim to be a "middle child", none of them can declare it quite like me. However, even though I am the fifth child, I believe that the life lessons and experiences that my siblings and I shared growing up in this family are consistent amongst one another. Over my 30 years, I have learned some valuable life lessons from my parents and siblings, and while I cannot begin to tell them all, these are just a few of the precious memories I have from being a part of this family.

Growing up, my siblings and I were not always afforded the opportunity to do all of the things that our friends did. We did not always have the chance to visit our friends at their houses or have them come over to our house. But, who needed that when there were always five to nine children already at home?

With so many children in the house, there was never a dull moment, unless we were sleep. Even then, that wasn't always a guarantee. For example, there was a time my three sisters and I decided to build a tent in our room. Growing up, the four of us shared one room. We went from having one queen size bed, sleeping head-to-toe, to having our own beds. Thanks to Da, who built three sets of bunk beds. We had two sets of bunk beds in the same room, of course. Well, one evening, we decided to make a tent in our room to sleep under. Our tent consisted of draping a comforter over the top posts of the two bunk beds and on the top of the mirror on the dresser. That was a great idea and actually lasted for a few minutes until the weight of the comforter caused the mirror to come crashing down! Even though the glass of the mirror did not break, the wood from the top of the mirror did. Ma and Da were not too happy about that; and, needless to say, that was the last tent that was built in our room.

Along with the ongoing excitement that comes from being in this family, the previous example also reminds me of the importance of discipline. Some parents think that they have to let their children do whatever they want, or they withhold discipline so that their children will like them and not be mad at them. Well, I am here to say that, when my parents disciplined me, I may not have liked them then, but now, I surely appreciate what they did for me. It is because of their discipline; that I am the woman that I am today.

Christmas time in our house was always an enjoyable occasion, a very exciting time, and a great learning experience for all of us; teaching us to always appreciate what you have no matter how great or small it may seem. Although there were nine children, Ma and Da found their rhythm for how to make Christmas work for their family.

Every year on Christmas Eve, we all had to "put out our shoes" (tradition similar to hanging out your stocking) to claim our spot in the living room. Knowing that Santa was not real, we knew Ma and Da would be the ones delivering things while we were sleeping. Well, at least they thought we were sleeping. We could hear them walking back and forth from their room to the living room and sometimes could even see them through the crack of our bedroom door. Not to mention, they would not let us go into their room a few days to a week before Christmas because we knew they had stuff hidden in their closet.

At any rate, 12:00 a.m. Christmas morning was always exciting, locating your shoes to see what you had in your spot! Even with nine children, my parents had done it again; everyone had something in their spot. No one had more than the other did. We received things we needed and things we wanted. We all were happy. After the excitement had settled, a couple of hours later, we would wake up again between 8:00 a.m. and 10:00 a.m. Dabbling in the gifts we had already viewed, we would gather around in the living room to do our gift exchange. We couldn't buy gifts for everyone; because that was too much buying! Therefore, with a gift exchange, we only had to buy a gift for the name we had picked. After that, we finally got to the heart of the day, our family talk and prayer. This was our moment to reflect on our time together as a family and to talk about the real meaning of Christmas, Christ's birth.

As the years went by and we got older, Christmas changed. The gifts and things we received on Christmas day grew less and less. Even though we didn't get a lot of stuff on Christmas day, there was never a day during the year that we needed something and my parents said, "Wait until Christmas." However, one thing remained the same, and still does now, and that is our prayer and family time. Now, even with no gifts under the Christmas tree, I'm more excited to go home for the holidays than ever before. Along with celebrating the birth of Christ this season, one of the lessons I have learned over the years is that it is not about what you get or what you can give to someone at this time of the year, but more about getting to spend time with family. Being older now, it is harder to get nine adults ... nine working adults ... some with families, some in other parts of the states and some in other states ... together all at the same time. However, Christmas is a time when we all can look forward to being together, and that is exciting.

In addition to learning how to appreciate what we have, another thing I've learned from being a part of this family is how to appreciate all the time we have together, whether it's the whole lot of us or just a few of us. I have been in the position before when my whole family has been together, except me, and it was not a good feeling. I have also been afforded the opportunity to spend some time alone with just my parents, which I would classify as golden times. I learn so much from them and realize that they really take the time out to care for each of us as individuals and not classify us as "just one of the nine."

Through the years, I sometimes have felt like it was hard making my own marks being the fifth child. I always found myself following the footsteps of the older four, always being referred to as "Q's little sister" or "little Sawyer" or "one of the Connie Bonnies." Even though they are not bad steps to follow or negative references, it was hard to be known as Crystal. However, I believe I have done well for myself, as I was the first female, of my siblings and cousins, from both sides of my parent's families to leave home and go off to college. Although some may have doubted me, today I hold two bachelor's degrees and a master's degree.

From my parents, I have learned that you have to strive for your best because no one else can or will do it for you. While journeying through high school, I did not know that not going to college was an option until one of my classmates mentioned he was not going. My parents did not force us to further our education by going to college. It was just instilled in us to strive for more. I just knew that, after high school, next came college. Before getting to that stage of my life, there were numerous examples of times I was pushed to strive harder. For example, I remember bringing home my report card from school one day and showing my mom the 96 I had made in one of my classes. Excited and proud of me, she said, "Good job! But you can bring it up." Not to lessen what I had accomplished, but in that moment, my mom encouraged me then not to settle for what I had received but to strive to do better. (She would also say that same comment if I showed her a 100!)

Receiving constant motivation from my parents has caused me to excel in my educational journey. I graduated #6 in my high school class. Four years later, I graduated from the University of North Carolina at Chapel Hill with a double major in Exercise and Sports Science and Psychology. Three years later, I graduated from Virginia Commonwealth University with a Master of Science in Occupational Therapy (OT). I now hold multiple OT licenses, allowing me to practice OT in various states.

Regardless of what life brings my way, I am truly grateful to be a part of my family and would not have it any other way. I often think of what it would be like if I were an only child or if there were less than nine of us, and I cannot imagine not having any of my siblings. While being the "true" middle child was not always the "ideal" spot for me, I feel like I was the only one who was able to spend an equal amount of time growing up with all of my siblings, from the oldest to the youngest. Even though I may feel stuck in the middle at times, I am still able to learn from all of my siblings. We all have been through different things in life, and, through it all, we have each other to learn from and lean on.

So, I think I speak for one through nine when I say that I am truly grateful and thankful to be a part of this family.

Fun facts:

- There are 12 ½ years between the oldest and youngest child.
- The largest age difference between any two siblings is 23 months.
- The smallest age difference between any two siblings is 14 months.
- There are four children with the 19th as their birth date.
- Connie: Josh –22 months apart
- Josh: Quinton – 16 months apart
- Quinton: Portia – 23 months apart
- Portia: Crystal – 21 months apart
- Crystal: Kellie –14 months apart
- Kellie: Anthony –15 months apart
- Anthony: Bonney –16 months apart
- Bonney: Raymond – 23 months apart

Patrick Mbai Chifunda

Being from Africa and living in America has presented various challenges for me. One of the many challenges I have faced is being away from my family. I left home at the age of 14 to pursue my career of becoming a professional squash player; and have since, traveled all over the world.

I am one of seven children. Our parents taught us the importance of family relationships; whether near or far. When I met Crystal, one of the first things I learned about her was that she was from a large family. As I got to know her and her family, I could see that we shared many of the same family values. This has been very comforting for me.

The family values I appreciate are the love for God, love and care for family, the importance of family time, work ethics, education, and a genuine care for others. I have lost both of my parents and there have been some difficult times. But, by being connected with the Sawyer family, I have gained more parents. I just want to encourage everyone to appreciate and value the time you have to spend with your parents and family members. Appreciate them while you can; because, you never know when the time will run out. I am so thankful to be connected with the Sawyer family as I continue to learn and grow in life.

Kellie Nicole Sawyer

The summer following my freshman year in high school, I attended a summer camp in Greenville, North Carolina, that targeted minority students and exposed them to various careers in the Allied Health field. There I was introduced to occupational therapy. At that point, I knew that I wanted a career in health care, and thought that I wanted to be a physical therapist. However, once I learned about OT and how it focuses on giving people the ability to live independent lives; I knew that was what I wanted to do with my life. From that moment to this point, I focused my energy on realizing that dream. I graduated high school as #6 in my class in June 2004 and graduated with my BA in Exercise and Sports Science in May 2008. I completed my graduate studies in occupational therapy at James Madison University in December 2010. I successfully completed my certification exam and have been practicing as an OT since January of 2011.

During one of our many sibling conference calls, Q reminds us not to forget to write the chapter for the book. What should I include? Those significant moments in our childhood which helped to progress us to this point in our lives?

First of all, what family requires a conference call to stay connected? That would be us. Upon recollection, what is it that makes us so, for the lack of a better word, different? I mean, to us, our lives were quiet and normal, except it was not. I can't count the number of times I was asked, "You have eight brothers and sisters? And you all have the same parents?" All this time, we thought we were the norm. We turned out to be the exception. Two- parent household: strong black male as a father figure and the head of the household; an exceptional mother who held it down on the home front; and nine high school graduates and nine college graduates. We have evolved into a family of young black professionals. How did we get there? Why are we so blessed?

Prayer

Without failing, before getting on the school bus, we would all stand in the hallway outside of our parent's room. Ma would usually read us a daily devotion from Guidepost or her little black book of devotions. She or Da would pray. Everyone would say a memory verse. We all would recite Philippians 4:13 together. And then, our trademark ending to anything, you guessed it, "Who do you love? Jesus!" Some days, we would almost miss the school bus to finish up our devotions.

On a side note, you got one chance to get out of the bed when Ma called for you. The second time around, she would come with a not so pleasant surprise. One way I used to escape was to fall on my knees and "pretend" to pray. I would be asleep, but when she came back around, I would say, "But I'm praying." It worked every time. Lord, forgive me …and Momma, forgive me too.

Love

Anyone with siblings knows the unwritten rule that siblings can fight amongst each other. But letting somebody else mess with them is a major problem. To this day, there are times when we don't see eye to eye on certain situations. However, our parents instilled in us a sense of love that can't be broken no matter what we are faced with. In addition, our life experiences as children strengthened our familial bond. Only we are aware of what it feels like labeled as a "Connie Bonnie", or identified as a number rather than a name. ("Hey number 6!"). We were viewed as the "goody goodies" amongst our family. Often, we felt left out. Of course, no harm was intended. That doesn't change the fact that it hurt.

However, this hurt enabled us to create a bond that can't be easily tampered with or broken.

Favor

I can't count the number of times we have said amongst each other, "Favor ain't fair." The thing is we really aren't so extra smart or filthy rich, which caused us to be in this position. God chose to favor my father, for whatever reason, and as a direct result, his favor has fallen on us because we are his direct seed. Nothing we have done has placed us in a position of "entitlement". Why God chose us, I will never know, but I'm grateful that He did.

CHAPTER 9

Reflections from the Legacy Sharers

We have heard from the oldest six children, as well as my children by marriage. In this last chapter of reflections, we want to hear from my three babies. We will get reflections from the youngest three children. I call them the legacy sharers because they received what the whole family had to offer in the legacy of love.

Anthony LaMarr Sawyer

My first name is Anthony, but my surname, Sawyer, is definitely the name that people recognize me by most often. Sawyer is the name that I was destined to have before I was ever born. It wasn't until recently that I realized just what it meant to be a part of this family. I am the seventh of the nine children that were born to Connie and Bonnie Sawyer. Somehow, I grew up thinking that being a part of a family this large was the norm; my father is the third of nine living children, and my mother is the youngest of nine children herself. In any case, if you get to know me at any level, the first thing that you'll discover is that I'm from a large family, and I love it. If you talk to me a little more, you will then discover that I am exceedingly and abundantly blessed because I am a part of this family.

Growing up, I knew that we weren't rich by any means; however, we never wanted for anything. My father was the breadwinner, driving two hours or more each day to work a job in another state. He never complained, and always showed me what it meant to be the man of the house. While he was at work, my mom took care of the house. When growing up and people asked what my mom did, I would usually respond that she was "the mother of nine"; the questions typically stopped after that. To be clear, the term "homemaker" doesn't really do my mother justice. She was first an example of what it meant to be a woman of God; and then she helped us to be respectful, responsible, obedient, and accountable. Growing up, my siblings, cousins, and I participated in a singing group called "The Children of God". My mother was our pianist, and my grandmother, "Grandma Shirley", was the leader over us all. Through this group and through the church, we gained the biblical foundation that we still use today.

I'm not really sure how to put into words how awesome God has been to my family and me; he has blessed us all in so many ways, and He continues to prove himself daily in my life. From my rural upbringing, I've traveled around the country and the world, meeting other people and gaining experiences that have helped to shape me into the man I am. Whether bungee jumping off a bridge in Zambia, experiencing a safari in Botswana, snorkeling in the US Virgin Islands, exploring underwater caves in Belize, or working in an impoverished area of New Orleans, I've experienced much in such a short period. However, I can never forget God, who made it all possible, and my family, who has supported me and uplifted me through it all.

Just like my siblings, I received my primary and secondary educations in the public school system in Camden, North Carolina. From kindergarten to fourth grade, I attended Grandy Primary School. I spent the next four years of my education at Camden Middle School and finished up at Camden County High School. These years of education were marked by a few major themes: parents who prepared my siblings and me for school before the year ever started, teachers who were truly invested in our success, and many opportunities for leadership roles and extracurricular activities. I left high school as valedictorian, class president, and the recipient of the Robertson Scholarship, which would finance four years of education at UNC. As a Robertson scholar, my tuition, room, board, and other expenses was covered. Additionally, I was granted the opportunity to take courses and live for a semester at Duke University. What's more, I was granted the opportunity to travel during each summer of my collegiate career.

During my first summer, I worked at Belle Reve, an HIV/AIDS house in New Orleans. The next summer, I volunteered at McCord Hospital, a semi-private hospital in Durban, South Africa, which serves a significant number of HIV-positive patients in the KwaZulu-Natal province. My final summer, I served as an administrative intern at Novant Health Matthews Medical Center – formerly Presbyterian Hospital Matthews – which is a small community hospital in a suburb of Charlotte, North Carolina. My college years and summer experiences were all in preparation for my greatest challenge to date: serving as a high school geometry and algebra teacher in Greenville, Mississippi as part of the Teach for America program. My two years in the classroom were the hardest of my life, but the experience of teaching in one of the highest need areas of the country is one that was invaluable, and the experience will certainly stick with me for the rest of my life.

In the fall of 2012, I began medical school at the University of Michigan as a recipient of the Dean's Merit Scholarship. Out of my entering cohort of 177 students, I was the only Black male. While this realization made me feel isolated at times, I entered into medical school with an enthusiasm that I had never experienced before: I was one step closer to being able to fulfill my passion. In addition to my studies, I served as an honor council representative, class advocate, admissions ambassador, president of our Black Medical Association, and treasurer of the Health Equity Scholars Program. I also volunteered with the Galens Medical Society, including as a participant in our annual Tag Days fundraiser that raises tens of thousands of dollars annually for children's charities in Washtenaw County, and as a producer for the 99th Annual Galens Smoker, a musical roast of the medical school faculty which involves over 100 students from across the medical school. My third year of medical school was especially enlightening, as my clinical experiences helped to confirm for me that I wanted to practice medicine as a pediatric anesthesiologist.

Becoming a physician is a goal that I have had for as long as I can remember, and I am extremely thankful that God has set me on a path that will see this dream become a reality. However, I also knew that I would not ultimately find contentment if my impact were limited to one patient at a time. In returning to my public health roots, I decided to take a year off from medical school to head to the Harvard T.H. Chan School of Public Health. During this year, I earned a masters of public health with a concentration in health policy. The Zuckerman Fellowship Program, administered through the Harvard Kennedy School's Center for Public Leadership, provided very generous support for this additional year of studies, and I am incredibly grateful for the opportunity to learn alongside such a distinguished group of scholars. Upon my completion of graduate and medical school in 2017, I moved to California to begin my residency as a transitional intern at Santa Clara Valley Medical Center, with plans to subsequently begin anesthesiology residency at Stanford in 2018. My goal is to work towards a career as both a clinician and a policy maker that focuses on health disparities and children's health policy.

I know that without God, nothing in my life would be possible. Also, I know that the support of my family is second to none. I am so grateful to be a part of the Sawyer Family.

Bonney LaBelle Sawyer Burton - Finding Love in a Hopeless Place

Love.... This word takes on different meanings to different people during different situations, right? Is love truly a noun or a verb? Well, I love the food I eat! Yet, I love the passion I feel toward my husband. I also feel butterflies in my stomach each time I hear my sons say "I love you". Do I really and truly have the right definition of what love is? I have been through several phases of "love" during my lifetime, but it was the love that I received from a seemingly hopeless place, that caused me to change my views on what love really was all about.

My name is Bonney LaBelle Burton. I had the honor of being named after my mother. The story has been told many times about how my mother had given birth to seven children and said, "If the next one is a girl, I'm going to get me a junior out of the deal!" And so it was, I was a girl, born three days before my mother's birthday. I was given not only her name, but also her sweet smile, and her love for singing. As a child, I remember being very happy and full of joy. Playing outside with my shoes off and attempting to plant apple seeds in our gravel driveway are some of my fondest memories. Making up songs was another memory that will never leave my mind. I would work hard on my newest lyrics, and then sing my heart out throughout the house. My siblings' response to my newest song was, "Ma, please make her stop!" Then they would approach me themselves and say "Shut up!" (of course, they couldn't say it too loud because we were not allowed to say "shut up"). My mother would simply say, "Just let her sing' and after having approval from my mother I would continue singing over my siblings' groans and obvious disapprovals.

During this time of my life I was a free spirit with a sweet smile on my face, an innocent "egg" released into the world. Being loved during this time of my life meant being prayed for, having food, clothes, and shelter, and knowing that I was not alone. Family always surrounded me and that made me feel secure. I knew I was loved because I felt it.

As I went through my "caterpillar" phase I enjoyed staying at my Godparents' house and spending time with my Grandmother, Shirley. Being in the company of adults who were not as strict as my parents but still made my well-being a priority gave me a safe haven. God and church were always a big deal in my family. As a child, I was part of a singing group called "The Children of God." My Grandma Shirley had the vision and with the help of my mother, the vision was put into action. I remember spending many school nights and weekends with my siblings and cousins practicing, rehearsing, and preparing for ministry. Many times, as we traveled to various locations, it was said that we were a saved bunch of children. As I reflect on those years, I did not know how to live saved or what it truly meant. However, there was a level of respect that I had for the adults in my life that just wouldn't allow me to do certain things. I was raised in the church and was taught at an early age the differences between what is right and wrong. My caterpillar stage was coming to an end and I had eaten all that I could before my point of explosion. At this point, love was taught to me. The simple scripture, "God is Love" 1 John 4:8, put love into perspective. I was told I was a child of God so I had to have love in my heart. Even with each mistake that I made, I always remembered that God is the first true example of showing love.

As I transitioned into my teenage years, I also transitioned into my cocoon, the chrysalis stage. I entrapped myself in my personal cocoon, a separate world of my own. I began doing things the way I wanted to and not considering God, my family, or the things I had "eaten" and learned during my caterpillar stage. I began finding enjoyment in things that did not align with the values and morals that were taught to me as a child. No longer was I concerned with others, I simply focused on myself. I began to rebel. Each detail of my rebellion would be enough to write a book of my own. I lied to my parents, snuck out the house, contemplated running away, and did not care what anyone had to say about it. I remember my siblings telling me that I needed to listen and respect my parents, but I just didn't care.

On October 26, 2007, I remember walking into my parents' bedroom and saying goodbye to them before leaving for school. I was preparing to play in the third round of the state -playoff for my volleyball team. It was my senior year, and I was so excited. My mother said to me, "Make sure you pray before you leave", so I did! Less than two minutes from my house, I was involved in a head-on collision. Needless to say, I did not make it to my volleyball game that evening. I broke my arm, fractured my ankle, and I got cut up pretty bad; but I was still alive.

Like I said earlier, during this phase of my life, I could only see myself. Although there were several underlying factors that affected me, I held my destiny. At this point, I fell deeply in love with my soul mate, R.J. It was through him that I learned how to love for real. Our relationship started in a somewhat hopeless place. Things that occurred before we established our relationship began to affect us in a negative way. However, we always found a way to see past the negative and keep our love for each other our number one priority.

It was hard to feel the love from my parents and even siblings because in their eyes, I was wrong and I needed to stop loving R.J. Even though I knew in my heart what type of person R.J. was and the way he made me feel, I began seeking love in different places. There were other guys along the way that I tried to "fall" for, but it never worked. R.J. was special to me and in the face of all adversity, I never let him go. With R.J., love came so naturally. He showed me that love was not about how much money you had, how popular you were, how well you played a sport, or how attractive you were. With R.J. love was feeling safe, being a good person, laughing, watching movies, and eating good food. These simple things were enough for me. I didn't have to be another person when I was with R.J. I was free to be me and I knew that I was loved because he reminded me of it often, not only with his words but also through his actions toward me. My choice to continue loving R.J. caused so much tension in my relationship with my parents and siblings but I didn't care! I was in love for the first time in my life and I never wanted to lose that feeling of excitement I felt each time I knew I would be around him.

Several very special people watched over me as I was in my chrysalis. My Grandmother Shirley played a significant role in this phase because she shared wisdom, showed compassion and understanding. Yet, she never passed judgment. Another person who made this phase of my life more bearable was R.J.'s mother, Wanda. Mrs. Wanda was so special to me because she always treated me as if I were her own daughter. She provided wisdom, comfort, and safety. She always had an open door and cared for me no matter what anyone else had to say about it. I learned more about myself during this long phase of self-reflection. Through trial and error, I found out my purpose and what I would and would not let control my life. I am not perfect, but I know that with God ALL THINGS ARE POSSIBLE!!!

After high school, I still wasn't sure what I wanted for my life. Again, I found myself in a somewhat hopeless place, because my plans for college were not working out the way I wanted and I was about to be separated from the person I loved most. Ultimately, I stayed close to home and attended Elizabeth City State University. There, I was part of the first cohort of Viking Fellows Teaching Scholars. This program was very similar to the North Carolina Teaching Fellows program. I had a full scholarship for college and even though I wanted to be as far away from home as possible, I was excited to know I would not have any college loans. As time went on, I felt so accomplished when I won first place in a writing contest and also when I was chosen to work in the Chancellor's office for a work study position. I began feeling more at ease and started meeting new people. R.J. was always on my mind but the distance did not help our relationship flourish.

During my second year of college, I had one of the biggest blessings and reality checks of my life: ASHETON! R.J. and I had our first son together. I experienced so many different emotions and contemplated doing so many different things during this time. I wanted to quit school and just care for my baby. After thinking a lot, I discovered that I would only be doing my baby a disservice by quitting. I had someone else depending on me and I couldn't fail him. With much hard work and prioritizing my life, I was able to graduate on time and with honors. I was hired as a third-grade teacher soon after graduation and began my career as an elementary school teacher. R.J. and I got engaged and life and love for me were going wonderfully. At times I became very complacent with who I was and where I was in life. I let my guard down on things that I shouldn't have and I gained weight and stopped focusing on things that were most important. I was simply going through the motions of my life.

On my wedding day, my father escorted me down the aisle. To be honest, I did not always feel that he would be walking me down the aisle on my wedding day. My relationship with my father was like a landslide. What started off on a strong foundation, gradually fell apart. The fall happened over time and it felt to me as if it were irreparable. I was "daddy's baby girl". I sat next to him at the dinner table, cleaned off his dresser so I could get the spare change, and even ironed all his handkerchiefs for work. I saw him as the man who would always love me no matter what. As I grew up, I started to grow apart from my father. Many of the things I did made him unhappy, but I didn't care. I knew what I wanted and if he told me I couldn't I went out of my way to show him how well I could really do it. I rebelled against him because I felt like he didn't understand what I was going through. I would voice my opinion over and over, and fail to get through to him every time. Over time, we found a way to get through all the misunderstanding and rebuild our relationship. Today I can say that I love my father and I have forgiven him. I know he has forgiven me, too. It is so different having an adult relationship with my father versus the relationship we had when I was a child. Now, we are able to laugh and joke with each other and talk about life. At times, I cause him to just shake his head and bite his bottom lip (to try to hold back his laughter) because of the unexpected things I say or do. That's the joy in how this situation worked out, I know my dad loves me unconditionally. I am thankful that my father was there to walk me down the aisle and I would not have had it any other way.

From my wedding day on, R.J. and I have learned so much more about one another. The first year of marriage truly will make or break you. You find out so many new things about one another. Some are special and intriguing, while others make you want to turn and run away. I have found that it is the true love that we have for each other that keeps us together. Laughing, learning, and loving are the things that consume the negative things that could possibly ruin our good thing.

During my third year of marriage, with the help of God, I was released from my cocoon. I began to spread my wings and show the world my true beauty. Now I do not look for validation from anyone else but God. I am a free spirit with a wild heart. God has blessed R.J. and me with two uniquely amazing boys, Asheton, and Carter. They both find a way to impact our lives for the better and they continue to challenge us to be better individuals. Through my personal experience, I learned that as a parent you have to trust your children when they make their "own" decisions. Once you have instilled the word of God in them, loved them without limitations, and given guidance on right and wrong, you must let go and trust God. Be mindful of what you say and how you say it; because once words are spoken you can never change them. Remember where you came from and what you have been through, it happened for a reason. Always pray for your children and be a living example for them. Create an open line of communication free of assumptions and judgment. Remember, even when it doesn't seem like it, your children hear what you say and what is in them will not leave. God is real and can handle any situation. He has the final say so. In the words of a song composed by my mother, "If you're gonna pray, don't worry. 'Cause, if you're gonna worry, why pray?"

Love God, love yourself, love your family, and love life.
Allow today to be a better day than yesterday.

As I continue to flourish into a better woman, I still continue to look around and I am in awe of God's glory. As I reflect, I realize that everything happens for a reason. I do not do much singing outwardly, but the song that I will continue to sing within is, "Amazing Grace shall always be my song of praise, for it was grace that brought my liberty ..." Even though you will not find me singing in a choir, I am thankful for the music God has put in my children's heart and it reminds me of my childhood each time I hear my boys singing at the top of their lungs. Through all the rough times and misunderstandings, R.J. and I found our true love out of a hopeless place. I would be remiss if I did not take the time to give a very special thank you to my husband, R.J. Yes, I did it; I saved the best part of my story for last.

RJ Burton

R.J. thank you for looking past the fat, fuzzy caterpillar that I was when we met in Ms. Nowell's third-grade class. Thank you for not leaving me even when I was blinded by my self-entrapment during our high school years. Thank you for being so patient during my transition from a young naïve lady to a wiser, more understanding woman. Now that you have helped me to know what love is and I love who I am, I know you will cherish my radiant beauty as you always have. You have proven yourself to me and I thank God for you each day. You have taught me how to love with my whole heart and without any limitations. Through you, I have learned how to be free and comfortable with who I am. I would not be who I am today if you had not been by my side through it all. I have not forgotten what you have been to me and what you have done for me. You truly complete me and I look forward to spending forever with you. I love you dearly R.J.

-B

Love is an action word. Have you been intentional
in showing the people around you how much you really love them?

Raymond Donnell Sawyer

I've accomplished quite a few things in my young life: I've captained varsity sports teams in high school, I've battled AIDS in an African country, I've spent a semester studying in Europe, and I've been a leader in Greek letter organizations. I've had dinners with millionaires, I've conversed with a Supreme Court Justice, I've shaken the hand of a five-star general, and I've even met the first African-American president of the United States and have the photo to prove it. Without a doubt, I've been blessed, and I have learned a lot through my experiences.

However, none of these experiences taught me more than my month-long backpacking expedition in the Northern Talkeetna Mountains of Alaska. Hiking through this uncultivated territory definitely pushed me physically, but it challenged me mentally on an entirely different level. I learned the true value of my family, both collectively and as individual members. After weeks in the wilderness with no electronics, running water, or even a pillow, nature was my only outlet. And it was then that I began to see my family, the ones that I care about the most, epitomized in nature, God's playground.

I thought of my father as the mountains. They are what make the overall scenery out there; they are what make Alaska. They are the rock, the foundation of the landscape, just like my father is the foundation of the family. Without the mountains, Alaska is just another place. Without him, we are just an ordinary family, not the extraordinary, unique, blessed, and favored family that we are. I thank God for giving him the ability to stand tall and be strong.

I viewed my mother as the water. Whether it's water from a lake, stream, creek, or river, water out there represents life. I could only camp near water; and camp provides some sort of comfort, stability, and rest. That's what my mother is. She is our source of life. Of course, we would not exist without her; and many times, when we feel we can't make it, she refreshes us with her love and words of wisdom. I thank her for being that essential resource we need to live.

The blue sky made me think of Connie III. As the first child, he set the bar of achievement so high for us; and by his example, he showed the younger siblings that the sky is the limit to what we can do and who we can be. I thank him for dreaming big and then working to reach his goals.

I discovered a giant feather one day, which reminded me of Joshua. I presume that the feather came from a bird, which, in the wilderness, provides the music. This particular feather looked as if it came from a large bird, the minister of music if you will. That's Josh. When it comes to the soundtrack of our family, he is the chief musician, making sure that we are in harmony with one another. He does those small things that mean so much. Simply eating Sunday dinner with my parents while many of us live away from home is a clear indication that he is committed to ensuring that the rhythm of life we experienced in the days of our youth will never be lost.

When there is a mountainside covered in loose rock, hikers call that talus; and for some reason, this relates to my brother, Quinton. Talus is some of the most difficult terrains to go over in the backcountry, and I feel like he has done some of the most difficult things in his young life. I understand how hard it must have been for him to move to Louisiana all by himself, and now to Michigan, but he had the big picture in mind. Just like I knew that crossing the talus was something I had to do in order to reach my campsite, he knew that the trials he faced would only lead him closer to his success in the future. I have the utmost respect for him.

The mountain peak is the best-suited reference for my sister, Portia. On select occasions throughout my wilderness experience, I was able to fully scale a mountain. The top is a place so many people long to be. They long for the beautiful view it possesses, but they fail to realize the true difficulty and struggle of getting to the top of that mountain. Portia is the mountain peak I see, and every day I recognize and appreciate the trials that she goes through to stay on that peak. She works hard to be the outstanding mother, daughter, auntie, sister, and friend that she is.

While in Alaska, we were required to hike from location to location in order for a bush plane to be able to land and resupply us with food and the other necessities for us to complete our journey. That bush plane describes Crystal. Every time I saw this plane, it was just like Christmas time. I was so happy to have some more food to eat, to get re-rationed. I feel like every time my family sees Crystal, our sense of family and unity and love is renewed, we are re-rationed by her spirit.

Rather than make campfires each time we prepared to cook, during my hiking days, we carried a small stove with us. That stove made me think of Kellie. Not just because she is uncontested in her ability to make a kitchen sing praises of heavenly aromas anytime she sees fit, but it was much deeper than that. In the mountains, the stove represents meals, which are your source of nourishment and recuperation after a long and weary journey. There have been several occasions where I have talked to Kellie, and her words of encouragement were the perfectly balanced meal that I needed to give me the ability to go on in life.

Trekking poles are items many experienced hikers use in their expeditions, so I just assumed that maybe they would help me too. Turns out those trekking poles helped me to hike over 100 miles of terrain, and saved my knees from tremendous pain in the process. That's what my brother, Anthony, has done for me. He has been a great example for me, helping me to get where I am today. He showed me a lot of the things he has encountered so that I could save myself some pain in my quest to achieve some of the successes he has already obtained. Though we fought consistently as adolescents because I was his copycat, I'm glad he let me stick around long enough to learn so much from him. I am truly blessed to have him as a big brother.

It may seem like a simple play on words, but my sister, Bonney, is truly the sun of the family. Her personality can brighten up so many dark places when she lets it. The sun didn't shine so often in the rainy climate of Alaska, but when it did, it made my day so much better. I don't truly get to spend as much time with Bonney as I used to, but whenever I get the opportunity, it's such a great thing because she lightens up my gloomy situations.

I didn't know it until I got there, but Alaska has a naturally growing blueberry population in those mountains. It may sound strange, but the blueberries reminded me of my two sisters-in-law, Alicia and Sh'Rhonda. The blueberries were the most pleasant surprise to my trip. I never thought about having blueberries on my hiking trip, but they were such a great addition to the meals. Growing up, I never really thought about having sisters-in-law, but those two gals are a tremendous asset to us. I constantly thank them for sweetening up our lives.

In Alaska, I had no cell phone, no computer, no Xbox, no music—nothing. My main source of entertainment was going to the lake to skip rocks. Doing that made me think of my nephews, and all the fun I have with them. Whether it's wrestling or throwing the Frisbee, I cherish the time I get to spend with them and invest in them, knowing that they will one day be the great men that will help carry on our family legacy.

Every beautiful flower that I saw reminded me of my nieces: Tiana, Leasia, Amaya, Nia, Janae, and Lauryn. Every time I came across a flower, I thought it was the most beautiful thing I had ever seen, - but then I would come across another one. It seems like every time I see my nieces, they are getting prettier and older and taking on the character of their wonderful mothers. I know they have to get old sometime, and I'm praying that God helps me to deal properly with the first young lad who calls and asks to speak to them.

Finally, I saw myself. I am Alaska, but you must understand that Alaska isn't just a name. It's really the mountains and lakes, the rivers and flowers, and all the other beautiful things that make it what it is. Without all these things Alaska would be just an insignificant place. That's me. Without my family, I am just any ole' person; I am another John Doe. They are what make me special. They, through the grace of God, have made me the person who I am.

I'm constantly asked what it's like to be the baby of the family, and so I must officially address it. Being the youngest child is the easiest -- and the hardest thing I've ever had to do. It's easy because if I want to be successful, I just have to watch the eight great examples before me. My brothers have shown me how a real man carries himself, and my sisters have demonstrated the qualities that I should desire in a future mate. They would advise me on what to expect during my first days with a new teacher, and they would give me the heads up on my new sports coaches. I never had to worry about being bullied in school, because everybody knew that I had an army supporting me.

However, it's quite difficult as well. I'm constantly faced with the challenge of walking in the colossal shoes left by my successful siblings. Whenever I walked into a class on the first day of school, I was always greeted with the phrase, "Oh yes, you're _____'s little brother." And with that came the monumental expectations of excellence. I often found myself becoming a copycat, adopting pieces of each of their personalities and fusing them into my own. This was both an asset and a liability. I had discovered a system that was successful, but I didn't want to be complacent with just being someone's little brother. I had to discover that I must take the mentorship and advice of my family, and use it as I strive to do great and newer things. It's not easy, by no extent of the imagination, but it's a challenge that I am willing to accept each day of my life, and I would have it no other way.

THE LEGACY CONTINUES

Sharing our legacy of love has taken me longer than it should have. Please forgive me. Our legacy is an ongoing saga. Noteworthy events occur almost daily. To endeavor to include every event would leave this book unfinished. Much has been included. However, it is impossible to include every detail

The timeline for our offerings spans over a decade. Much of what was written, was before recent events in our family. Since beginning work on the book, babies have been born and we have celebrated marriages. If the flow of events seems a little disjointed, that's why.

I will endeavor to keep you with an update on my blog. Feel free to visit there with any questions, comments, or concerns. I would love to hear from each and every one of you. Again, my blog address is: **blessed2bbndsawyer.wordpress.com**

Remember...

You should now see how a legacy of love has come out of the life of my family. When heaven holds the destiny of your child, expect God's plans for purpose to be fulfilled. I hope we have encouraged your hearts through this humble offering.

In conclusion, remember the following:

- God must always be first.
- Implement educational things to challenge young minds.

- Engage in conversations about life.
- Recognize communication as the thin line between understanding and misunderstanding.
- Think about the consequences of your actions.
- Understand that unity breeds strength, power, victory, and hope.
- Walk together.
- Encourage one another.
- Remind one another that you can make it.
- Believe that the thing the devil designed for your demise will catapult you into God's expected end for you… victory! In fact, the thing that the devil designed to take you out will literally push you into an end greater than what was before.
- Receive all that you need from the Lord. God will deliver what you need to progress.
- Respect leadership.
- Honor the elderly.
- Support the youth.
- Always give God thanks, honor, and praise.

I pray that this labor of love has been a blessing to all the readers. I love you all. Thank you for sharing with the Connie and Bonnie Sawyer family. God keep you in His love and care. Be blessed!

Raymond -Connie, Jr. Bonnie -Connie, III Alicia Lauryn Connie, IV -Joshua Sh'Rhonda Tiana Jashon Janae - Q Lauren -Portia Leasia Amaya Nia -Crystal Patrick -Kellie -Anthony -Bonney RJ Asheton Carter

Connie & Shirley Sawyer, Sr. Melvin & Mamie Downing, Sr.

2015

97

I was asked why I wanted to include so many pictures. I actually included just a few. The saying, "a picture is worth a thousand words" inspired me. There's no way I can write all that I feel about family unity and real family love ties. I see so much in the pictures. Hopefully, you can, too ... the smile, the touch, the closeness, laughter, tears, hope, excitement, history, celebration, togetherness, devotion, faith, adventure, legacy, love ...

family photos

Bonnie & Connie, Jr.

Connie, III, Joshua, Q, Anthony, Raymond

NINE

Portia, Crystal, Kellie, Bonney

Connie, III   Kellie   Anthony

Portia   Raymond   Crystal

Quinton   Bonney   Joshua

Connie, III, Lauryn, Wil, Alicia

Lauren, Q

Anthony, Kellie, Raymond

Carter, RJ, Asheton, Bonney

FAM
(Family Always Matters)

Patrick, Crystal

Jashon, Joshua, Sh'Rhonda, Janae, Tiana

Nia Portia, Amaya, Leasia

great-grandparents
Connie, Sr. & Shirley

grandchildren

(pictured L to R)
Tiana, Leasia
Carter, Wil, Asheton, Jashon
Amaya, Lauryn, Janae, Nia

Connie Wildred Sawyer, Sr.
Connie Wildred Sawyer, Jr.
Connie Wildred Sawyer, III
Connie Wildred Sawyer, IV

The CbSawyer family had seven participants in the UNC band for seventeen consecutive years. Wow! Half-time recognition at a UNC football game. Thank you Jeff, El, Leon, and all who made November 24, 2012, a memorable day for the CbSawyer family. The announcer even shared why Q was not able to join us on this occasion. Thank you, Jennifer, for doing such an amazing job capturing this moment in time. Our gift, a framed picture of the old well, has a place of honor in our Carolina blue living room.

(pictured L to R)

Raymond, RJ, Bonney, Asheton, Anthony, Kellie, Crystal, Patrick, Leasia, Nia, Portia, Amaya, Tiana, Sh'Rhonda, Jashon, Joshua, Janae, Alicia, Lauryn, Connie, III, Bonnie, Connie, Jr.

blessed to be …

(pictured, L to R)

+ Connie W. Sawyer, III: Attorney & Alicia J. Sawyer: Commercial Real Estate Paralegal

+ Joshua D. Sawyer: Math Teacher & Sh'Rhonda J. Sawyer: Income Maintenance Caseworker

+ Quinton L. Sawyer: Athletic Trainer in NBA & Lauren C. Sawyer: PR Manager

+ Portia Z. Parker: Administrative Intern

+ Crystal S. Chifunda: Occupational Therapist & Patrick M. Chifunda: Professional Squash Coach

+ Kellie N. Sawyer: Occupational Therapist

+ Anthony L. Sawyer - Physician

+ Bonney L. Burton: Elementary Teacher & RJ Burton: 1st Lieutenant United States Army

+ Raymond D. Sawyer: Channels Specialist for Google

CbSawyer Family Vacation 2017 in Gatlinburg, TN.
All present except one.

(pictured, L to R)

Anthony, Kellie, Q, Lauren, Bonnie, Connie, Jr., Crystal, Patrick, Portia,
Raymond, Alicia, Connie, III, Joshua, Jashon, Nia, Leasia,
Carter, Bonney, Asheton, Wil, Lauryn, Sh'Rhonda, Tiana, Janae, Amaya

**We missed having you with us RJ
However, we understand that when
duty calls, you must answer.**

21-DAYS DEVOTIONAL

(Pictured L to R)
Connie, Jr., Bonnie, Connie, III, Alicia, Joshua, Sh'Rhonda, Q,
Portia, Crystal, Kellie, Anthony, Bonney, Raymond

I reached a point in my life where things looked bleak and felt overwhelming. What I was experiencing, was similar to what some of my loved ones could have been experiencing. In other words, it was the difference between reading about struggles and living the struggle. Can I be transparent? Thank you! Really, the bill was due, and I didn't know where the money was going to come from. In the midst of every struggle, God must still be first. Do I or should I pay tithes and cheerfully giving an offering when I'm in the middle of a financial lack. Yep! I give to God first, off the top, and not as an afterthought with whatever is left over. I believe God and I believe what the Word says. However, many times I need to be strengthened in my faith. Anyway, I was at a point in my life where I felt like screaming for release. I know we quote scriptures after scripture after scripture. But, when real life hits you square in the face, attacking your faith, weakening your resolve, and distracting your focus; it's time to seek God, seek His face, ingest His Word, pray, and fast like never before.

Then I had an epiphany, a sudden realization. I needed my family to help strengthen me through the power of God's Word. It was very early in the morning when I cried out. I made my request known, and my family came through for me. Thus, for twenty-one days, my family sustained me through the power of God's Word, fasting and prayer. What I learned from this experience is to trust God completely. As long as I'm able to work out a situation, it's very easy to forget that God is still the one in charge. However, when I don't have; and the way is yet met, I know that my God is in control working it all out in my favor. I am blessed!

I debated within myself about including the following section. To include this section, won out. Reading all these scriptures at one time could be overwhelming. Therefore, I suggest you approach it as a daily devotional. Allow these scriptures to penetrate like a slow, steady rain. It is placed at the end of the book with the hope that you will take your time and enjoy these scriptures one day at a time. I promise, you will be blessed! There is power in the Word of God. I even thought about placing this devotional on my blog: *blessed2bbndsawyer.wordpress.com*. However, some of my readers may not know how to maneuver on the internet. It is important for me to share this time in my life where we shared scriptures with each other for strength and empowerment. We still do so, in measure (not everyone, everyday), to this present day.

Our means of communication was the Group Me app. Read, enjoy, and be blessed!

Day 1:
May 30, 2012, 12:40 a.m.

bndsawyer: I'm hungry. Family, for the next 21 days I need all of you, who will accept the plea, to feed me. My life, my sanity, my breakthrough is at stake. Each of you please send me one word daily. Please. I need you to pray and really seek God for what to share with me. I asked CC the other day what he would think if I just hollered. He told me to go ahead . . . and he hollered. He said I would feel better. I think Asheton shouted "Hallelujah!" Of course, I just kept everything inside. Well, I'm shouting now and I'm asking for help. I need your prayers, the Word, and for you to fast for me. Thank you in advance. If any Scripture is repeated, I will consider that God is trying to get my attention and confirm a particular truth. Sometimes a smile is used to camouflage the turmoil raging on the inside. I declare and decree that we (the CbSawyer Family) shall live and not die. Be blessed!

bndsawyer: I will bless the LORD at all times: his praise *shall continually be* in my mouth. Psalm 34:1

Anthony: Even the youths shall faint and be weary, and the young men shall utterly fall: But they that wait upon the LORD shall renew *their* strength; they shall mount up with wings as eagles; they shall run, and not be weary, *and* they shall walk, and not faint. Isaiah 40:30-31

Kellie: Ye are of God, little children, and have overcome them: because greater is he that is in you, than he that is in the world. I John 4:4

Thanks, Ma . . . I have no doubt we will all be empowered through this . . . much love to everyone

Sh'Rhonda Sawyer: Now the God of hope fill you with all joy and peace in believing, that ye may abound in hope, through the power of the Holy Ghost. Romans 15:13

Portia: I can do all things through Christ which strengtheneth me. Philippians 4:13

Raymond: But the Lord is faithful, who shall stablish you, and keep *you* from evil. II Thessalonians 3:3

Joshua: My brethren, count it all joy when ye fall into divers temptations; Knowing *this*, that the trying of your faith worketh patience. But let patience have *her* perfect work, that ye may be perfect and entire, wanting nothing. James 1:2-4

Connie, III: Worry weighs a person down; an encouraging word cheers a person up. Proverbs 12:25 (NLT)

Crystal: There hath no temptation taken you but such as is common to man: but God *is* faithful, who will not suffer you to be tempted above that ye are able; but will with the temptation also make a way to escape, that ye may be able to bear *it*. I Corinthians 10:13

Bonney: And let us not be weary in well doing: for in due season we shall reap, if we faint not. Galatians 6:9

Bonney: FYI . . . smiling also can show all the joy that is bundled up inside your soul . . . let your smile always represent your joy . . . I got my smile from you for a reason . . .

bndsawyer: Hallelujah! Word to the rescue! For 21 days . . . Oh, I know all is well. I am so for real. Thank you so much for loving and Wording me to life. I feel empowered.

Q: Beloved, let us love one another (love one a-no-o-o-ther): for love is of God; and every one that loveth is born of God, and knoweth God. He that loveth not knoweth not God; for God is love. (beloved, let us love one another) I John four seven and eight (clap clap clap clap) I John four seven and eight. From memory. Look what you did mama. Love you.

bndsawyer: Love you all. I'm so blessed!

Connie, Jr.: In the beginning was the Word, and the Word was with God, and the Word was God. But my God shall supply all your need according to His riches in glory by Christ Jesus.

bndsawyer: John 1:1; Philippians 4:19

Alicia: BE YE ANGRY, AND SIN NOT: let not the sun go down upon your wrath: Neither give place to the devil. Ephesians 4:26-27

bndsawyer: We did it, family. To God be the glory. 1/21 days! Hallelujah!

Day 2:
May 31, 2012, 2:01 a.m.

Crystal: Psalm 46:1-2a (NIV)

1 God is our refuge and strength, an ever-present help in trouble.

2 Therefore we will not fear . . .

Sh'Rhonda Sawyer: Humble yourselves therefore under the mighty hand of God, that he may exalt you in due time: Casting all your care upon him; for he careth for you. Be sober, be vigilant;

because your adversary the devil, as a roaring lion, walketh about, seeking whom he may devour: Whom resist stedfast in the faith, knowing that the same afflictions are accomplished in your brethren that are in the world. But the God of all grace, who hath called us unto his eternal glory by Christ Jesus, after that ye have suffered a while, make you perfect, stablish, strengthen, settle *you*. To him *be* glory and dominion for ever and ever. Amen. I Peter 5:6-11

Had to put it all

bndsawyer: Amen. Though I might also have confidence in the flesh. If any other man thinketh that he hath whereof he might trust in the flesh, I more: … Brethren, I count not myself to have apprehended: but *this* one thing *I do*, forgetting those things which are behind, and reaching forth unto those things which are before, I press toward the mark for the prize of the high calling of God in Christ Jesus. Philippians 3:4, 13-14

Kellie: I beseech you therefore, brethren, by the mercies of God, that ye present your bodies a living sacrifice, holy, acceptable unto God, *which is* your reasonable service. And be not conformed to this world: but be ye transformed by the renewing of your mind, that ye may prove what *is* that good, and acceptable, and perfect, will of God. Romans 12:1-2

Connie, III: But if we are living in the light, as God is in the light, then we have fellowship with each other, and the blood of Jesus, his Son, cleanses us from all sin. I John 1:7 (NLT)

Joshua: Now unto the King eternal, immortal, invisible, the only wise God, *be* honour and glory for ever and ever. Amen. I Timothy 1:17

Portia: Have not I commanded thee? Be strong and of a good courage; be not afraid, neither be thou dismayed: for the LORD thy God *is* with thee whithersoever thou goest. Joshua 1:9

Crystal: Idk about you ma . . . or anybody else but this is really blessing me!

Raymond: God *is* not a man, that he should lie; neither the son of man, that he should repent: hath he said, and shall he not do *it?* or hath he spoken, and shall he not make it good? Numbers 23:19

Bonney: Then he said unto them, Go your way, eat the fat, and drink the sweet, and send portions unto them for whom nothing is prepared: for *this* day is holy unto our Lord: neither be ye sorry; for the joy of the LORD is your strength. Nehemiah 8:10

Q: Nay, in all these things we are more than conquerors through him that loved us. For I am persuaded, that neither death, nor life, nor angles, nor principalities, nor powers, nor things present, nor things to come, Nor height, nor depth, nor any other creature, shall be able to separate us from the love of God, which is in Christ Jesus our Lord. Romans 8:37-39

Anthony: And he said unto me, My grace is sufficient for thee: for my strength is made perfect in weakness. Most gladly therefore will I rather glory in my infirmities, that the power of Christ may rest upon me. II Corinthians 12:9

Connie, Jr.: The LORD *is* my shepherd; I shall not want.

Alicia: He maketh me to lie down in green pastures: he leadeth me beside the still waters. He restoreth my soul: he leadeth me in the paths of righteousness for his name's sake. Yea, though I walk through the valley of the shadow of death, I will fear no evil: for thou *art* with me; thy rod and thy staff they comfort me. Thou preparest a table before me in the presence of mine enemies: thou anointest my head with oil; my cup runneth over. Surely goodness and mercy shall follow me all the days of my life: and I will dwell in the house of the LORD for ever. Psalm 23

Alicia: Whither shall I go from thy spirit? or whither shall I flee from thy presence? If I ascend up into heaven, thou *art* there: if I make my bed in hell, behold, thou *art there. If* I take the wings of the morning, *and* dwell in the uttermost parts of the sea; Even there shall thy hand lead me, and thy right hand shall hold me. Psalm 139:7-10

Connie, Jr.: Thank you, Alicia.

Alicia: My pleasure!

bndsawyer: For I know the thoughts that I think toward you, saith the LORD, thoughts of peace, and not of evil, to give you an expected end. Then shall ye call upon me, and ye shall go and pray unto me, and I will hearken unto you. And ye shall seek me, and find *me*, when ye shall search for me with all your heart. Jeremiah 29:11-13

bndsawyer: Thou wilt keep *him* in perfect peace, *whose* mind *is* stayed *on thee*: because he trusteth in thee. Trust ye in the LORD for ever: for in the LORD JEHOVAH *is* everlasting strength: Isaiah 26:3-4

Day 3:
June 1, 2012, 4:26 a.m.

Kellie: Blessed *is* the man that walketh not in the counsel of the ungodly, nor standeth in the way of sinners, nor sitteth in the seat of the scornful. But his delight *is* in the law of the LORD; and in his law doth he meditate day and night. And he shall be like a tree planted by the rivers of water, that bringeth forth his fruit in his season; his leaf also shall not wither; and whatsoever he doeth shall prosper. Psalm 1:1-3

Sh'Rhonda Sawyer: He hath not dealt with us after our sins; nor rewarded us according to our iniquities. For as the heaven is high above the earth, *so* great is his mercy toward them that fear him. As far as the east is from the west, *so* far hath he removed our transgressions from us. Psalm 103:10-12

Connie, III: Fire tests the purity of silver and gold, but the LORD tests the heart. Proverbs 17:3 (NLT)

Connie, III: Grandchildren are the crowning glory of the aged; parents are the pride of their children. Proverbs 17:6 (NLT)

Connie, III: Loving Proverbs right now . . .

Joshua: Be careful for nothing; but in every thing by prayer and supplication with thanksgiving let your requests be made known unto God. And the peace of God, which passeth all understanding, shall keep your hearts and minds through Christ Jesus. Philippians 4:6-7

Joshua: We gotta pray just to make it today

Alicia: If ye walk in my statutes, and keep my commandments, and do them; Then I will give you rain in due season, and the land shall yield her increase, and the trees of the field shall yield their fruit. And your threshing shall reach unto the vintage, and the vintage shall reach unto the sowing time: and ye shall eat your bread to the full, and dwell in your land safely. Leviticus 26:3-5

Bonney: Thou wilt keep *him* in perfect peace, *whose* mind *is* stayed *on thee*: because he trusteth in thee. Isaiah 26:3

Portia: But ye, beloved, building up yourselves on your most holy faith, praying in the Holy Ghost, Keep yourselves in the love of God, looking for the mercy of our Lord Jesus Christ unto eternal life. And of some have compassion, making a difference: And others save with fear, pulling *them* out of the fire; hating even the garment spotted by the flesh. Now unto him that is able to keep you from falling, and to present *you* faultless before the presence of his glory with exceeding joy, To the only wise God our Saviour, *be* glory and majesty, dominion and power, both now and ever. Amen. Jude 20-25

Portia: Thanks mom for inspiring me to dig deeper. One day I will share my story. Love y'all.

Anthony: To appoint unto them that mourn in Zion, to give unto them beauty for ashes, the oil of joy for mourning, the garment of praise for the spirit of heaviness; that they might be called trees of righteousness, the planting of the LORD, that he might be glorified. Isaiah 61:3

Anthony: For when you're going through something.

Q: O God, thou *art* my God; early will I seek thee: my soul thirsteth for thee: my flesh longeth for thee in a dry and thirsty land, where no water is; To see thy power and thy glory, so *as* I have seen thee in the sanctuary. Because thy lovingkindness *is* better than life, my lips shall praise thee. Psalm 63:1-3

Kellie: Again Ma, thank you . . . this has been AWESOME to me!!!

Connie, Jr.: O taste and see that the LORD *is* good: blessed *is* the man *that* trusteth in him. Psalm 34:8

Raymond: Fear thou not; for I *am* with thee: be not dismayed; for I *am* thy God: I will strengthen thee; yea, I will help thee; yea, I will uphold thee with the right hand of my righteousness. Behold, all they that were incensed against thee shall be ashamed and confounded: they shall be as nothing; and they that strive with thee shall perish. Thou shalt seek them, and shalt not find them, *even* them that contended with thee: they that war against thee shall be as nothing, and as a thing of nought. For I the LORD thy God will hold thy right hand, saying unto thee, Fear not; I will help thee. Isaiah 41:10-13

Crystal: Matthew 7:6-8

6 Give not that which is holy unto the dogs, neither cast ye your pearls before swine, lest they trample them under their feet, and turn again and rend you.

7 Ask, and it shall be given you; seek, and ye shall find; knock, and it shall be opened unto you:

8 For every one that asketh receiveth; and he that seeketh findeth; and to him that knocketh it shall be opened.

Bonney: Crystal were you at church last night? The preacher preached about that! GOD is working on me.

Crystal: Wow! No sis I wasn't and I had no idea . . . woke up w it in my spirit this am as I was praying for what verse to send . . . wow, thank you, Jesus!

Day 4:
June 2, 2012, 5: 48 a.m.

Connie, III: But who am I, and who are my people, that we could give anything to you? Everything we have has come from you, and we give you only what you first gave us! I Chronicles 29:14 (NLT)

Connie, III: I know this is a random one, but if you ever get to read the entire chapter, it's David praising God in the midst of preparing the temple and his acknowledging God's favor in choosing His people to do this work. Deep stuff . . .

Joshua: But my God shall supply all your need according to his riches in glory by Christ Jesus. Philippians 4:19

Sh'Rhonda Sawyer: And the LORD answered me, and said, Write the vision, and make *it* plain upon tables, that he may run that readeth it. For the vision *is* yet for an appointed time, but at the end it shall speak, and not lie: though it tarry, wait for it; because it will surely come, it will not tarry. Habakkuk 2:2-3

Kellie: Create in me a clean heart, O God; and renew a right spirit within me. Cast me not away from thy presence; and take not thy holy spirit from me. Restore unto me the joy of thy salvation; and uphold me *with thy* free spirit. *Then* will I teach transgressors thy ways; and sinners shall be converted unto thee. Psalm 51:10-13

Portia: But I will hope continually, and will yet praise thee more and more. My mouth shall shew forth thy righteousness *and* thy salvation all the day; for I know not the numbers *thereof.* I will go in the strength of the Lord GOD: I will make mention of thy righteousness, *even* of thine only. Psalm 71:14-16

Anthony: For I know the thoughts that I think toward you, saith the LORD, thoughts of peace, and not of evil, to give you an expected end. Jeremiah 29:11

Crystal: Exodus 14:13-14

13 And Moses said unto the people, Fear ye not, stand still, and see the salvation of the LORD, which he will shew to you to day: for the Egyptians whom ye have seen to day, ye shall see them again no more for ever.

14 The LORD shall fight for you, and ye shall hold your peace.

Q: Wherefore I put thee in remembrance that thou stir up the gift of God, which is in thee by putting on of my hands. For God hath not given us the spirit of fear; but of power, and of love, and of a sound mind. II Timothy 1:6-7

Raymond: The LORD *is* my light and my salvation; whom shall I fear? The LORD *is* the strength of my life; of whom shall I be afraid? Psalm 27:1

Connie Jr.: I will bless the LORD at all times: his praise *shall* continually *be* in my mouth. O magnify the LORD with me and let us exalt his name together. Psalm 34:1, 3

bndsawyer: I must work the works of him that sent me, while it is day: the night cometh, when no man can work. John 9:4

Alicia: The fear of the LORD *is* the beginning of knowledge: *but* fools despise wisdom and instruction. Proverbs 1:7

Day 5:
June 3, 2012, 6:05 a.m.

Connie III: People may be right in their own eyes, but the LORD examines their heart. The LORD is more pleased when we do what is right and just than when we offer him sacrifices. Proverbs 21:2-3 (NLT)

Raymond: Delight thyself also in the LORD; and he shall give thee the desires of thine heart. Commit thy way unto the LORD; trust also in him; and he shall bring *it* to pass. And he shall bring forth thy righteousness as the light, and thy judgment as the noonday. Psalm 37:4-6

Bonney: ...God hath not given us the spirit of fear ... II Timothy 1:7a

Crystal: Joshua 1:7-8 (NIV)

7 Be strong and very courageous. Be careful to obey all the law my servant Moses gave you; do not turn from it to the right or to the left, that you may be successful wherever you go.

8 Keep this Book of the Law always on your lips; meditate on it day and night, so that you may be careful to do everything written in it. Then you will be prosperous and successful.

Connie, Jr.: I will bless the LORD at all times: his praise *shall* continually *be* in my mouth. My soul shall make her boast in the LORD: the humble shall hear *thereof*, and be glad. O magnify the LORD with me, and let us exalt his name together. Psalm 34:1-3

Sh'Rhonda Sawyer: And let us not be weary in well doing: for in due season we shall reap, if we faint not. Galatians 6:9

Q: ...God is love. I John 4:8b

Anthony: To every *thing there is* a season, and a time to every purpose under the heaven: A time to be born, and a time to die; a time to plant, and a time to pluck up *that which is* planted; A time to kill, and a time to heal; a time to break down, and a time to build up; A time to weep, and a time to laugh; a time to mourn, and a time to dance; A time to cast away stones, and a time to gather stones together; a time to embrace, and a time to refrain from embracing; A time to get, and a time to lose; a time to keep, and a time to cast away; A time to rend, and a time to sew; a time to keep silence, and a time to speak; A time to love, and a time to hate; a time of war, and a time of peace. Ecclesiastes 3:1-8

Bonney: ... all have sinned, and come short of the glory of God; Romans 3:23

Joshua: Humble yourselves therefore under the mighty hand of God, that he may exalt you in due time: Casting all your care upon him; for he careth for you. I Peter 5:6-7

bndsawyer: Be careful for nothing; but in every thing by prayer and supplication with thanksgiving let your requests be made known unto God. Philippians 4:6

Alicia: Iron sharpeneth iron; so a man sharpeneth the countenance of his friend. Proverbs 27:17

Kellie: Go to now, ye that say, To day or to morrow we will go into such a city, and continue there a year, and buy and sell, and get gain: Whereas ye know not what *shall be* on the morrow. For what *is* your life? It is even a vapour, that appeareth for a little time, and then vanisheth away. For that ye *ought* to say, If the Lord will, we shall live, and do this, or that. James 4:13-15

Portia: Thou therefore endure hardness, as a good soldier of Jesus Christ. No man that warreth entangleth himself with the affairs of *this* life; that he may please him who hath chosen him to be a soldier. II Timothy 2:3-4

Day 6:
June 4, 2012, 5:40 a.m.

Sh'Rhonda Sawyer: Let no man despise thy youth; but be thou an example of the believers, in word, in conversation, in charity, in spirit, in faith, in purity. I Timothy 4:12

Raymond: Trust in the LORD with all thine heart; and lean not unto thine own understanding. In all thy ways acknowledge him, and he shall direct thy paths. Proverbs 3:5-6

Joshua: Ray, I had to speak yesterday and that was one of the scriptures I referred to

Joshua: For I reckon that the sufferings of this present time *are* not worthy *to be compared* with the glory which shall be revealed in us. Romans 8:18

Kellie: ... for the record, Josh went IN on that bass yesterday . . . and his boo did her thing as well . . .

Kellie: And we know that all things work together for good to them that love God, to them who are the called according to *his* purpose. Romans 8:28

This is my favorite verse of all time . . . there's a reason I reply to everything with "it's all good"

Joshua: Yes she did . . . We have to learn to praise until the earthquake comes and shakes up everything that had us bound . . . She started to hoop a little bit too.

Portia: Create in me a clean heart, O God; and renew a right spirit within me. Cast me not away from thy presence; and take not thy holy spirit from me. Restore unto me the joy of thy salvation; and uphold me *with thy* free spirit. *Then* will I teach transgressors thy ways; and sinners shall be converted unto thee. Psalm 51:10-13

Bonney: And be ye kind one to another, tenderhearted, forgiving one another, even as God for Christ's sake hath forgiven you. Ephesians 4:32

Anthony: Who shall separate us from the love of Christ? *shall* tribulation, or distress, or persecution, or famine, or nakedness, or peril, or sword? As it is written, FOR THY SAKE WE ARE KILLED ALL THE DAY LONG; WE ARE ACCOUNTED AS SHEEP FOR THE SLAUGHTER. Nay, in all these things we are more than conquerors through him that loved us. For I am persuaded, that neither death, nor life, nor angels, nor principalities, nor powers, nor things present, nor things to come, Nor height, nor depth, nor any other creature, shall be able to separate us from the love of God, which is in Christ Jesus our Lord. Romans 8:35-39

Q: The Lord *is* my rock, and my fortress, and my deliverer; my God, my strength, in whom I will trust; my buckler, and the horn of my salvation, *and* my high tower. Psalms 18:2

Connie, III: I have hidden your word in my heart, that I might not sin against you. Your word is a lamp to guide my feet and a light for my path. Psalm 119:11, 105 (NLT)

Connie, Jr.: The LORD *is* my shepherd; I shall not want. He maketh me to lie down in green pastures: he leadeth me beside the still waters. He restoreth my soul: he leadeth me in the paths of righteousness for his name's sake. Psalm 23:1-3

bndsawyer: Now unto him that is able to keep you from falling, and to present *you* faultless before the presence of his glory with exceeding joy, To the only wise God our Saviour, *be* glory and majesty, dominion and power, both now and ever. Amen. Jude 24-25

Crystal: I Chronicles 16:34-35

34 O give thanks unto the LORD; for *he is* good; for his mercy *endureth* for ever.

35 And say ye, Save us, O God of our salvation, and gather us together, and deliver us from the heathen, that we may give thanks to thy holy name, *and* glory in thy praise.

Alicia: But the fruit of the Spirit is love, joy, peace, longsuffering, gentleness, goodness, faith, Meekness, temperance: against such there is no law. Galatians 5:22-23

Day 7:
June 5, 2012, 5:47 a.m.

Sh'Rhonda Sawyer: Wisdom *is* the principal thing; *therefore* get wisdom: and with all thy getting, get understanding. Proverbs 4:7

Kellie: And I will remember my covenant, which *is* between me and you and every living creature of all flesh; and the waters shall no more become a flood to destroy all flesh. And the bow shall be in the cloud; and I will look upon it, that I may remember the everlasting covenant between God and every living creature of all flesh that *is* upon the earth. Genesis 9:15-16

Raymond: Finally, my brethren, be strong in the Lord, and in the power of his might. Put on the whole armour of God, that ye may be able to stand against the wiles of the devil. For we wrestle not against flesh and blood, but against principalities, against powers, against the rulers of the darkness of this world, against spiritual wickedness in high *places*. Ephesians 6:10-12

Connie, III: The LORD our God has secrets known to no one. We are not accountable for them, but we and our children are accountable forever for all that he has revealed to us, so that we may obey all the terms of these instructions. Deuteronomy 29:29 (NLT)

Portia: Lift up your heads, O ye gates; and be ye lift up, ye everlasting doors; and the King of glory shall come in. Psalm 24:7

Q: Every word of God *is* pure: he *is* a shield unto them that put their trust in him. Proverbs 30:5

Anthony: Trust in the LORD, and do good; *so* shalt thou dwell in the land, and verily thou shalt be fed. Delight thyself also in the LORD; and he shall give thee the desires of thine heart. Commit thy way unto the LORD; trust also in him; and he shall bring it to pass. Psalm 37:3-5

bndsawyer: What time I am afraid, I will trust in thee. In God I will praise his word, in God I have put my trust; I will not fear what flesh can do unto me. Psalm 56:3-4

Joshua: Thou wilt keep *him* in perfect peace, *whose* mind *is* stayed *on thee*: because he trusteth in thee. Isaiah 26:3

Bonney: … weeping may endure for a night, but joy *cometh* in the morning. Psalms 30:5b

Connie, Jr.: But what saith it? THE WORD IS NIGH THEE, *EVEN* IN THY MOUTH, AND IN THY HEART: that is, the word of faith, which we preach; That if thou shalt confess with thy mouth the Lord Jesus, and shalt believe in thine heart that God hath raised him from the dead, thou shalt be saved. For with the heart man believeth unto righteousness; and with the mouth confession is made unto salvation. For the scripture saith, WHOSOEVER BELIEVETH ON HIM SHALL NOT BE ASHAMED. Romans 10:8-11

Alicia: Better *is* the end of a thing than the beginning thereof: *and* the patient in spirit *is* better than the proud in spirit. Ecclesiastes 7:8

Crystal: Let the words of my mouth, and the meditation of my heart, be acceptable in thy sight, O Lord, my strength, and my redeemer. Psalms 19:14

Day 8:
June 6, 2012, 5:31 a.m.

Sh'Rhonda Sawyer: Now faith is the substance of things hoped for, the evidence of things not seen. Hebrews 11:1

Connie, III: No one has ever seen God. But if we love each other, God lives in us, and his love is brought to full expression in us. And God has given us his Spirit as proof that we live in him and he in us. I John 4:12-13 (NLT)

Joshua: And the lord said unto the servant, Go out into the highways and hedges, and compel *them* to come in, that my house may be filled. Luke 14:23

Kellie: LORD, how are they increased that trouble me! Many *are* they that rise up against me. Many *there be* which say of my soul, *There is* no help for him in God. Selah. But thou, O LORD, *art* a shield for me; my glory, and the lifter up of mine head. Psalm 3:1-3

Portia: The LORD *is* my light and my salvation; whom shall I fear? The LORD *is* the strength of my life; of whom shall I be afraid? When the wicked, *even* mine enemies and my foes, came upon me to eat up my flesh, they stumbled and fell. Psalm 27:1-2

Raymond: Nay, in all these things we are more than conquerors through him that loved us. Romans 8:37

Connie, Jr.: Wherefore seeing we also are compassed about with so great a cloud of witnesses, let us lay aside every weight, and the sin which doth so easily beset *us*, and let us run with patience the race that is set before us, And ye have forgotten the exhortation which speaketh unto you as unto children, MY SON DESPISE NOT THOU THE CHASTENING OF THE LORD, NOR FAINT WHEN THOU ART REBUKED OF HIM: FOR WHOM THE LORD LOVETH HE CHASTENETH ... Hebrews 12:1, 5-6a

bndsawyer: The LORD will give strength unto his people; the LORD will bless his people with peace. Psalm 29:11

But the salvation of the righteous *is* of the LORD: *he is* their strength in the time of trouble. Psalm 37:39

Anthony: And they brought young children to him, that he should touch them: and *his* disciples rebuked those that brought *them*. But when Jesus saw *it*, he was much displeased, and said unto them, Suffer the little children to come unto me, and forbid them not: for of such is the kingdom of God. Mark 10:13-14

Q: Thou wilt keep *him* in perfect peace, *whose* mind *is* stayed *on thee*: because he trusteth in thee. Trust ye in the LORD for ever: for in the LORD JEHOVAH *is* everlasting strength: Isaiah 26:3-4

Bonney: You will make your prayer to him, and he will hear you; and you will pay your vows. Job 22:27 (RSV)

Crystal: So shall my word be that goeth forth out of my mouth: it shall not return unto me void, but it shall accomplish that which I please, and it shall prosper *in the thing* whereto I sent it. Isaiah 55:11

Day 9:
June 7, 2012, 5:34 a.m.

Sh'Rhonda Sawyer: For I know the thoughts that I think toward you, saith the LORD, thoughts of peace, and not of evil, to give you an expected end. Jeremiah 29:11

Kellie: But seek ye first the kingdom of God, and his righteousness; and all these things shall be added unto you. Take therefore no thought for the morrow: for the morrow shall take thought for the things of itself. Sufficient unto the day *is* the evil thereof. Matthew 6:33-34

Anthony: Many *are* the afflictions of the righteous: but the LORD delivereth him out of them all. Psalm 34:19

Connie, III: How great is our Lord! His power is absolute! His understanding is beyond comprehension! Psalm 147:5 (NLT)

Raymond: Are not two sparrows sold for a farthing? and one of them shall not fall on the ground without your Father. But the very hairs of your head are all numbered. Fear ye not therefore, ye are of more value than many sparrows. Matthew 10:29-31

Portia: My brethren, count it all joy when ye fall into divers temptations; Knowing *this*, that the trying of your faith worketh patience. But let patience have *her* perfect work, that ye may be perfect and entire, wanting nothing. James 1:2-4

Q: Many sorrows *shall be* to the wicked: but he that trusteth in the LORD, mercy shall compass him about. Be glad in the LORD, and rejoice, ye righteous: and shout for joy, all *ye that are* upright in heart. Psalm 32:10-11

bndsawyer: In my distress I called upon the LORD, and cried to my God: and he did hear my voice out of his temple, and my cry *did enter* into his ears. II Samuel 22:7

Joshua: And let us not be weary in well doing: for in due season we shall reap, if we faint not. Galatians 6:9

bndsawyer: Yea, God! I believe your word! Bless your name, Jesus! Hallelujah!

Crystal: Philippians 4:4-6

4 Rejoice in the Lord alway: *and* again I say, Rejoice.

5 Let your moderation be known unto all men. The Lord *is* at hand.

6 Be careful for nothing; but in every thing by prayer and supplication with thanksgiving let your requests be made known unto God.

Alicia: He that spareth his rod hateth his son: but he that loveth him chasteneth him betimes. Proverbs 13:24

Connie, Jr.: FOR WHOSOEVER SHALL CALL UPON THE NAME OF THE LORD SHALL BE SAVED. Romans 10:13

Day 10
June 8, 2012, 5:54 a.m.

Sh'Rhonda Sawyer: For we have not an high priest which cannot be touched with the feeling of our infirmities; but was in all points tempted like as *we are, yet* without sin. Hebrews 4:15

Joshua: There hath no temptation taken you but such as is common to man: but God *is* faithful, who will not suffer you to be tempted above that ye are able; but will with the temptation also make a way to escape, that ye may be able to bear *it*. I Corinthians 10:13

Alicia: *There is* one body, and one Spirit, even as ye are called in one hope of your calling; One Lord, one faith, one baptism, One God and Father of all, who *is* above all, and through all, and in you all. But unto every one of us is given grace according to the measure of the gift of Christ. Ephesians 4:4 -7

Kellie: Seek ye the Lord while he may be found, call ye upon him while he is near: Isaiah 55:6

Crystal: Mark 10:29-31

29 And Jesus answered and said, Verily I say unto you, There is no man that hath left house, or brethren, or sisters, or father, or mother, or wife, or children, or lands, for my sake, and the gospel's,

30 But he shall receive an hundredfold now in this time, houses, and brethren, and sisters, and mothers, and children, and lands, with persecutions; and in the world to come eternal life.

31 But many *that are* first shall be last; and the last first.

Anthony: Whither shall I go from thy spirit? or whither shall I flee from thy presence? If I ascend up into heaven, thou *art* there: if I make my bed in hell, behold, thou *art there. If* I take the wings of the morning, *and* dwell in the uttermost parts of the sea; Even there shall thy hand lead me, and thy right hand shall hold me. Psalm 139:7-10

Connie, III: As a dog returns to its vomit, so a fool repeats his foolishness. Proverbs 26:11 (NLT)

Raymond: And Jesus said unto them, Because of your unbelief: for verily I say unto you, If ye have faith as a grain of mustard seed, ye shall say unto this mountain, Remove hence to yonder place; and it shall remove; and nothing shall be impossible unto you. Matthew 17:20

Bonney: What time I am afraid, I will trust in thee. Psalm 56:3

Connie, Jr.: For that which I do I allow not: for what I would, that do I not; but what I hate, that do I. If then I do that which I would not, I consent unto the law that *it is* good. Now then it is no more I that do it, but sin that dwelleth in me. For I know that in me (that is, in my flesh,) dwelleth no good thing: for to will is present with me; but *how* to perform that which is good I find not.

For the good that I would I do not: but the evil which I would not, that I do. Romans 7:15-19

Q: Trust in the Lord with all your heart, and lean not on your own understanding; In all your ways acknowledge Him, and He shall direct your paths. Proverbs 3:5-6 (NKJV)

bndsawyer: And ye shall serve the LORD your God, and he shall bless thy bread, and thy water; and I will take sickness away from the midst of thee. Exodus 23:25

Portia: But if ye forgive not men their trespasses, neither will your Father forgive your trespasses. Matthew 6:15

Day 11:
June 9, 2012, 7:58 a.m.

Sh'Rhonda Sawyer: Delight thyself also in the LORD; and he shall give thee the desires of thine heart. Commit thy way unto the LORD; trust also in him; and he shall bring *it* to pass. And he shall bring forth thy righteousness as the light, and thy judgment as the noonday. Psalm 37:4-6

Crystal: And if it seem evil unto you to serve the LORD, choose you this day whom ye will serve; whether the gods which your fathers served that *were* on the other side of the flood, or the gods of the Amorites, in whose land ye dwell: but as for me and my house, we will serve the LORD. Joshua 24:15

Connie III: But Samuel replied, What is more pleasing to the LORD: your burnt offerings and sacrifices or your obedience to his voice? Listen! Obedience is better than sacrifice, and submission is better than offering the fat of rams. I Samuel 15:22 (NLT)

Kellie: Quinton got the spirit! Quench not the Spirit. I Thessalonians 5:19

Q: Yes, Lord! Might as well be me!

Connie, Jr.: Righteousness exalteth a nation: but sin *is* a reproach to any people. Proverbs 14:34

Anthony: If my people, which are called by my name, shall humble themselves, and pray, and seek my face, and turn from their wicked ways; then will I hear from heaven, and will forgive their sin, and will heal their land. II Chronicles 7:14

Joshua: Therefore if any man *be* in Christ, *he is* a new creature: old things are passed away; behold, all things are become new. II Corinthians 5:17

Alicia: For from the rising of the sun even unto the going down of the same my name *shall be* great among the Gentiles; and in every place incense *shall be* offered unto my name, and a pure offering: for my name *shall be* great among the heathen, saith the LORD of hosts. Malachi 1:11

Raymond: If ye shall ask any thing in my name, I will do *it*. John14:14

Raymond: Sh'Rhonda, that's my favorite scripture.

Bonney: Foolishness *is* bound in the heart of a child; *but* the rod of correction shall drive it far from him. Proverbs 22:15

Q: The LORD *is* good, a strong hold in the day of trouble; and he knoweth them that trust in him. Nahum 1:7

Portia: But many *that are* first shall be last; and the last first. Mark 10:31

bndsawyer: O give thanks unto the LORD, for *he is* good: for his mercy *endureth* for ever. Psalm 107:1

Day 12:
June 10, 2012, 12:16 a.m.

bndsawyer: But they that wait upon the LORD shall renew *their* strength; they shall mount up with wings as eagles; they shall run, and not be weary; *and* they shall walk, and not faint. Isaiah 40:31

Alicia: Let your light so shine before men, that they may see your good works, and glorify your Father, which is in heaven. Matthew 5:16

Connie, III: People who conceal their sins will not prosper, but if they confess and turn from them, they will receive mercy. Blessed are those who fear to do wrong, but the stubborn are headed for serious trouble. Proverbs 28:13-14 (NLT)

Sh'Rhonda Sawyer: And let us not be weary in well doing: for in due season we shall reap, if we faint not. Galatians 6:9

Joshua: I beseech you therefore, brethren, by the mercies of God, that ye present your bodies a living sacrifice, holy, acceptable unto God, *which is* your reasonable service. And be not conformed to this world: but be ye transformed by the renewing of your mind, that ye may prove what *is* that good, and acceptable, and perfect, will of God. Romans 12:1-2

Connie, Jr.: Wherefore take unto you the whole armour of God, that ye may be able to withstand in the evil day, and having done all, to stand. Stand therefore, having your loins girt about with truth, and having on the breastplate of righteousness; And your feet shod with the preparation of the gospel of peace; Above all, taking the shield of faith, wherewith ye shall be able to quench all the fiery darts of the wicked. And take the helmet of salvation, and the sword of the Spirit, which is the word of God: Praying always with all prayer and supplication in the Spirit, and watching thereunto with all perseverance and supplication for all saints; Ephesians 6:13-18

Kellie: This is THE STONE WHICH WAS SET AT NOUGHT OF YOU BUILDERS, WHICH IS BECOME THE HEAD OF THE CORNER. Neither is there salvation in any other: for there is none other name under heaven given among men, whereby we must be saved. Acts 4:11-12

Raymond: Therefore, my beloved brethren, be ye stedfast, unmoveable, always abounding in the work of the Lord, forasmuch as ye know that your labour is not in vain in the Lord. I Corinthians 15:58

Crystal: Habakkuk 2:2-3

2 And the Lord answered me, and said, Write the vision, and make *it* plain upon tables, that he may run that readeth it.

3 For the vision *is* yet for an appointed time, but at the end it shall speak, and not lie: though it tarry, wait for it; because it will surely come, it will not tarry.

Anthony: And Jabez called on the God of Israel, saying, Oh that thou wouldest bless me indeed, and enlarge my coast, and that thine hand might be with me, and that thou wouldest keep *me* from evil, that it may not grieve me! And God granted him that which he requested. I Chronicles 4:10

Q: Hold your peace, let me alone, that I may speak, and let come on me what *will*. Wherefore do I take my flesh in my teeth, and put my life in mine hand? Though he slay me, yet will I trust him: but I will maintain mine own ways before him. Job 13:13-15

Bonney: The lost sheep . . . find it and read it

Bonney: Matthew 18:10-14

Portia: The steps of a *good* man are ordered by the LORD: and he delighteth in his way. Though he fall, he shall not be utterly cast down: for the LORD upholdeth *him with* his hand. Psalm 37:23-24

Day 13:
June 11, 2012, 5:49 a.m.

Sh'Rhonda Sawyer: If we confess our sins, he is faithful and just to forgive us *our* sins, and to cleanse us from all unrighteousness. I John 1:9

Kellie: Now unto him that is able to do exceeding abundantly above all that we ask or think, according to the power that worketh in us, Ephesians 3:20

Connie, III: For everyone has sinned; we all fall short of God's glorious standard. Yet God, in his grace, freely makes us right in his sight. He did this through Christ Jesus when he freed us from the penalty for our sins. Romans 3:23-24 (NLT)

Connie, III: Or in KJV. . .

Connie, III: For all have sinned, and come short of the glory of God; being justified freely by his grace through the redemption that is in Christ Jesus: Romans 3:23-24

Joshua: How precious also are thy thoughts unto me, O God! how great is the sum of them! *If* I should count them, they are more in number than the sand: when I awake, I am still with thee. Psalm 139:17-18

Joshua: God thinks well of us . . . wow!

Raymond: And we know that all things work together for good to them that love God, to them who are the called according to *his* purpose. Romans 8:28

Anthony: My brethren, count it all joy when ye fall into divers temptations; Knowing *this*, that the trying of your faith worketh patience. But let patience have *her* perfect work, that ye may be perfect and entire, wanting nothing. James 1:2-4

Q: For I know the thoughts that I think toward you, saith the LORD, thoughts of peace, and not of evil, to give you an expected end. Then shall ye call upon me, and ye shall go and pray unto me, and I will hearken unto you. Jeremiah 29:11-12

Connie, Jr.: Children, obey your parents in the Lord: for this is right. HONOUR THY FATHER AND MOTHER; (which is the first commandment with promise;) THAT IT MAY BE WELL WITH THEE, AND THOU MAYEST LIVE LONG ON THE EARTH. Ephesians 6:1-3

Crystal: Psalms 34:13-14

13 Keep thy tongue from evil, and thy lips from speaking guile.

14 Depart from evil, and do good; seek peace, and pursue it.

bndsawyer: per Bonney's request: Take heed that ye despise not one of these little ones; for I say unto you, That in heaven their angels do always behold the face of my Father which is in heaven. For the Son of man is come to save that which was lost. How think ye? if a man have an hundred sheep, and one of them be gone astray, doth he not leave the ninety and nine, and goeth into the mountains, and seeketh that which is gone astray? And if so be that he find it, verily I say unto you, he rejoiceth more of that *sheep*, than of the ninety and nine which went not astray. Even so it is not the will of your Father which is in heaven, that one of these little ones should perish. Matthew 18:10-14

bndsawyer: Blessed *be* the LORD, because he hath heard the voice of my supplications. The Lord *is* my strength and my shield; my heart trusted in him, and I am helped: therefore my heart greatly rejoiceth; and with my song will I praise him. The LORD *is* their strength, and he *is* the saving strength of his anointed. Psalm 28:6-8

Alicia: Beloved, think it not strange concerning the fiery trial which is to try you, as though some strange thing happened unto you: But rejoice, inasmuch as ye are partakers of Christ's sufferings;

that, when his glory shall be revealed, ye may be glad also with exceeding joy. If ye be reproached for the name of Christ, happy *are ye*; for the spirit of glory and of God resteth upon you: on their part he is evil spoken of, but on your part he is glorified. But let none of you suffer as a murderer, or *as* a thief, or *as* an evildoer, or as a busybody in other men's matters. Yet if *any man suffer* as a Christian, let him not be ashamed; but let him glorify God on this behalf. For the time *is come* that judgment must begin at the house of God: and if *it* first *begin* at us, what shall the end *be* of them that obey not the gospel of God? I Peter 4:12-17

Bonney: My brethren, count it all joy when ye fall into divers temptations; Knowing *this*, that the trying of your faith worketh patience. James 1:2-3

Portia: Wait on the LORD: be of good courage, and he shall strengthen thine heart: wait, I say, on the LORD. Psalm 27:14

Day 14
June 12, 2012, 5:06 a.m.

bndsawyer: The Lord shall laugh at him: for he seeth that his day is coming. The steps of a *good* man are ordered by the LORD: and he delighteth in his way. Though he fall, he shall not be utterly cast down: for the LORD upholdeth *him with* his hand. I have been young, and *now* am old; yet have I not seen the righteous forsaken, nor his seed begging bread. Psalm 37:13, 23-25

bndsawyer: Let us be good.

Sh'Rhonda Sawyer: Seeing then that we have a great high priest, that is passed into the heavens, Jesus the Son of God, let us hold fast *our* profession. For we have not an high priest which cannot be touched with the feeling of our infirmities; but was in all points tempted like as *we are, yet* without sin. Let us therefore come boldly unto the throne of grace, that we may obtain mercy, and find grace to help in time of need. Hebrews 4:14-16

Kellie: Therefore it *is* of faith, that *it might be* by grace; to the end the promise might be sure to all the seed; not to that only which is of the law, but to that also which is of the faith of Abraham; who is the father of us all, (As it is written, I HAVE

MADE THEE A FATHER OF MANY NATIONS,) before him whom he believed, *even* God, who quickeneth the dead, and calleth those things which be not as though they were. Who against hope believed in hope, that he might become the father of many nations; according to that which was spoken, So shall thy seed be. And being not weak in faith, he considered not his own body now dead, when he was about an hundred years old, neither yet the deadness of Sara's womb: He staggered not at the promise of God through unbelief; but was strong in faith, giving glory to God; Romans 4:16-20

Connie III: That's the whole story. Here now is my final conclusion: Fear God and obey his commands, for this is everyone's duty. God will judge us for everything we do, including every secret thing, whether good or bad. Ecclesiastes 12:13-14 (NLT)

Alicia: And beside this, giving all diligence, add to your faith virtue; and to virtue knowledge; And to knowledge temperance; and to temperance patience; and to patience godliness; And to godliness brotherly kindness; and to brotherly kindness charity. For if these things be in you, and abound, they make *you that ye shall* neither *be* barren nor unfruitful in the knowledge of our Lord Jesus Christ. II Peter 1:5-8

Connie, Jr.: Beware of dogs, beware of evil workers, beware of the concision. But what things were gain to me, those I counted loss for Christ. Yea doubtless, and I count all things *but* loss for the excellency of the knowledge of Christ Jesus my Lord: for whom I have suffered the loss of all things, and do count them *but* dung, that I may win Christ, And be found in him, not having mine own righteousness, which is of the law, but that which is through the faith of Christ, the righteousness which is of God by faith: That I may know him, and the power of his resurrection, and the fellowship of his sufferings, being made conformable unto his death; Philippians 3:2, 7-10

Joshua: Study to shew thyself approved unto God, a workman that needeth not to be ashamed, rightly dividing the word of truth. II Timothy 2:15

Raymond: And he said unto me, My grace is sufficient for thee: for my strength is made perfect in weakness. Most gladly therefore will I rather glory in my infirmities, that the power of Christ may rest upon me. Therefore I take pleasure in infirmities, in reproaches, in necessities, in persecutions, in distresses for Christ's sake: for when I am weak, then am I strong. II Corinthians 12:9-10

Anthony: But without faith *it is* impossible to please *him*: for he that cometh to God must believe that he is, and *that* he is a rewarder of them that diligently seek him. Hebrews 11:6

Bonney: Let us be glad and rejoice, and give honour to him: for the marriage of the Lamb is come, and his wife hath made herself ready. Revelation 19:7

Q: One *thing* have I desired of the LORD, that will I Seek after; that I may dwell in the house of the Lord all the days of my life, to behold the beauty of the Lord, and to enquire in his temple. For in the time of trouble he shall hide me in his pavilion: in the secret of his tabernacle shall he hide me; he shall set me up upon a rock. Psalm 27:4-5

Crystal: Psalm 27:1-4

1 The LORD *is* my light and my salvation; whom shall I fear? The LORD *is* the strength of my life; of whom shall I be afraid?

2 When the wicked, *even* mine enemies and my foes, came upon me to eat up my flesh, they stumbled and fell.

3 Though an host should encamp against me, my heart shall not fear: though war should rise against me, in this *will* I be confident.

4 One *thing* have I desired of the Lord, that will I seek after; that I may dwell in the house of the Lord all the days of my life, to behold the beauty of the Lord, and to enquire in his temple.

Q: lol Crystal and I musta been on the same page lol

Crystal: Wow that's wassup . . . I didn't even read anyone else's before I sent my scripture lol

Portia: Another parable put he forth unto them, saying, The kingdom of heaven is like to a grain of mustard seed, which a man took, and sowed in his field: Which indeed is the least of all seeds: but when it is grown, it is the greatest among herbs, and becometh a tree, so that the birds of the air come and lodge in the branches thereof. Matthew 13:31-32

Portia: Don't count yourself out. God has a way of taking us little folks and making us into strong warriors for Him!

Q: Portia, that'll preach! Ay! 2, 3, GO!

Day 15:
June 13, 2012, 5:42 a.m.

Sh'Rhonda Sawyer: Ask, and it shall be given you; seek, and ye shall find; knock, and it shall be opened unto you: For every one that asketh receiveth; and he that seeketh findeth; and to him that knocketh it shall be opened. Matthew 7:7-8

Kellie: Not that I speak in respect of want: for I have learned, in whatsoever state I am, *therewith* to be content. I know both how to be abased, and I know how to abound: everywhere and in all things I am instructed both to be full and to be hungry, both to abound and to suffer need. Philippians 4:11-12

Connie, III: Every word of God proves true. He is a shield to all who come to him for protection. Do not add to his words, or he may rebuke you and expose you as a liar. Proverbs 30:5-6 (NLT)

Alicia: But, beloved, be not ignorant of this one thing, that one day *is* with the Lord as a thousand years, and a thousand years as one day. The Lord is not slack concerning his promise, as some men count slackness; but is longsuffering to us-ward, not willing that any should perish, but that all should come to repentance. II Peter 3:8-9

Joshua: Every good gift and every perfect gift is from above, and cometh down from the Father of lights, with whom is no variableness, neither shadow of turning. James 1:17

bndsawyer: I *am* the LORD: that *is* my name: and my glory will I not give to another, neither my praise to graven images. Behold, the former things are come to pass, and new things do I declare: before they spring forth I tell you of them. Isaiah 42:8-9

Raymond: Now the Lord of peace himself give you peace always by all means. The Lord *be* with you all. II Thessalonians 3:16

Anthony: Thou wilt keep *him* in perfect peace, *whose* mind *is* stayed *on thee*: because he trusteth in thee. Trust ye in the Lord forever: for in the Lord JEHOVAH is everlasting strength: Isaiah 26:3-4

Crystal: Psalm 119:10-11

10 With my whole heart have I sought thee: O let me not wander from thy commandments.

11 Thy word have I hid in mine heart, that I might not sin against thee.

Connie, Jr.: The earth *is* the Lord'S, and the fulness thereof; the world, and they that dwell therein. For he hath founded it upon the seas, and established it upon the floods. Who shall ascend into the hill of the Lord? or who shall stand in his holy place? He that hath clean hands, and a pure heart; who hath not lifted up his soul unto vanity, nor sworn deceitfully. He shall receive the blessing from the Lord, and righteousness from the God of his salvation. Psalm 24:1-5

Q: The Lord thy God in the midst of thee is mighty; he will save, he will rejoice over thee with joy; he will rest in his love, he will joy over thee with singing. Zephaniah 3:17

Bonney: In every thing give thanks: for this is the will of God in Christ Jesus concerning you. I Thessalonians 5:18

Portia: Thou believest that there is one God; thou doest well: the devils also believe, and tremble. But wilt thou know, O vain man, that faith without works is dead? James 2:19-20

Day 16:
June 14, 2012, 3:48 a.m.

Kellie: But thanks *be* to God, which giveth us the victory through our Lord Jesus Christ. Therefore, my beloved brethren, be ye stedfast, unmoveable, always abounding in the work of the Lord, forasmuch as ye know that your labour is not in vain in the Lord. I Corinthians 15:57-58

Connie, III: Sometimes something simply said is effective . . .

Connie, III: For the wages of sin is death, but the free gift of God is eternal life through Christ Jesus our Lord. Romans 6:23 (NLT)

Sh'Rhonda Sawyer: Brethren, if a man be overtaken in a fault, ye which are spiritual, restore such an one in the spirit of meekness; considering thyself, lest thou also be tempted. Bear ye one another's burdens, and so fulfil the law of Christ. For if a man think himself to be something, when he is nothing, he deceiveth himself. Galatians 6:1-3

Crystal: John 17:14-17

14 I have given them thy word; and the world hath hated them, because they are not of the world, even as I am not of the world.

15 I pray not that thou shouldest take them out of the world, but that thou shouldest keep them from the evil.

16 They are not of the world, even as I am not of the world.

17 Sanctify them through thy truth: thy word is truth.

Alicia: Better *is* a dry morsel, and quietness therewith, than an house full of sacrifices *with* strife. Proverbs 17:1

Anthony: But my God shall supply all your need according to his riches in glory by Christ Jesus. Philippians 4:19

Portia: Wherefore I say unto thee, Her sins, which are many, are forgiven; for she loved much: but to whom little is forgiven, *the same* loveth little. And he said unto her, Thy sins are forgiven. And they that sat at meat with him began to say within themselves, Who is this that forgiveth sins also? And he said to the woman, Thy faith hath saved thee; go in peace. Luke 7:47-50

Raymond: Stand fast therefore in the liberty wherewith Christ hath made us free, and be not entangled again with the yoke of bondage. Galatians 5:1

Joshua: Now unto him that is able to do exceeding abundantly above all that we ask or think, according to the power that worketh in us, Unto him *be* glory in the church by Christ Jesus throughout all ages, world without end. Amen. Ephesians 3:20-21

bndsawyer: Pray without ceasing. I Thessalonians 5:17

Be careful for nothing; but in every thing by prayer and supplication with thanksgiving let your requests be made known unto God. Philippians 4:6

Q: For I consider that the sufferings of this present time are not worthy *to be compared* with the glory which shall be revealed in us. For we were saved in this hope, but hope that is seen is not hope; for why does one still hope for what he sees? But if we hope for what we do not see, we eagerly wait for *it* with perseverance. Romans 8:18, 24-25(NKJV)

Connie, Jr.: Fret not thyself because of evildoers, neither be thou envious against the workers of iniquity. For they shall soon be cut down like the grass, and wither as the green herb. Trust in the LORD, and do good; *so* shalt thou dwell in the land, and verily thou shalt be fed. Delight thyself also in the LORD; and he shall give thee the desires of thine heart. Psalm 37:1-4

Bonney: The LORD *is* my shepherd; I shall not want. Psalm 23:1

Day 17:
June 15, 2012, 8:05 a.m.

Sh'Rhonda Sawyer: The LORD bless thee, and keep thee: The LORD make his face shine upon thee, and be gracious unto thee: The LORD lift up his countenance upon thee, and give thee peace. And they shall put my name upon the children of Israel; and I will bless them. Numbers 6:24-27

Joshua: If I shut up heaven that there be no rain, or if I command the locusts to devour the land, or if I send pestilence among my people; If my people, which are called by my name, shall humble themselves, and pray, and seek my face, and turn from their wicked ways; then will I hear from heaven, and will forgive their sin, and will heal their land. II Chronicles 7:13-14

Raymond: But the fruit of the Spirit is love, joy, peace, longsuffering, gentleness, goodness, faith, Meekness, temperance: against such there is no law. Gal. 5:22-23

Connie, III: And since we have a great High Priest who rules over God's house, let us go right into the presence of God with sincere hearts fully trusting him. For our guilty consciences have been sprinkled with Christ's blood to make us clean, and our bodies have been washed with pure water. Hebrews 10:21-22 (NLT)

Connie, III: And *having* an high priest over the house of God; Let us draw near with a true heart in full assurance of faith, having our hearts sprinkled from an evil conscience, and our bodies washed with pure water. Hebrews 10:21-22

Anthony: Hereby know ye the Spirit of God: Every spirit that confesseth that Jesus Christ is come in the flesh is of God: And every spirit that confesseth not that Jesus Christ is come in the flesh is not of God: and this is that *spirit* of antichrist, whereof ye have heard that it should come; and even now already is it in the world. Ye are of God, little children, and have overcome them: because greater is he that is in you, than he that is in the world. I John 4:2-4

Kellie: I will bless the LORD at all times: his praise *shall* continually *be* in my mouth. My soul shall make her boast in the LORD: the humble shall hear *thereof*, and be glad. O magnify the LORD with me, and let us exalt his name together. Psalm 34:1-3

bndsawyer: I will declare the decree: the Lord hath said unto me, Thou *art* my Son; this day have I begotten thee. Psalm 2:7

Alicia: The beginning of strife *is as* when one letteth out water: therefore leave off contention, before it be meddled with. Proverbs 17:14

Crystal: Psalm 61:1-4

1 Hear my cry, O God; attend unto my prayer.

2 From the end of the earth will I cry unto thee, when my heart is overwhelmed: lead me to the rock *that* is higher than I.

3 For thou hast been a shelter for me, *and* a strong tower from the enemy.

4 I will abide in thy tabernacle for ever: I will trust in the covert of thy wings. Selah.

Q: I beseech you therefore, brethren, by the mercies of God, that ye present your bodies a living sacrifice, holy, acceptable unto God, *which is* your reasonable service. Rejoicing in hope; patient in tribulation, continuing instant in prayer; Romans 12:1,12

Connie, Jr.: Except the LORD build the house, they labour in vain that build it: except the LORD keep the city, the watchman waketh *but* in vain. Lo, children *are* an heritage of the LORD: *and* the fruit of the womb *is his* reward. As arrows *are* in the hand of a mighty man; so *are* children of the youth. Happy *is* the man that hath his quiver full of them: they shall not be ashamed, but they shall speak with the enemies in the gate. Psalm 127:1, 3-5

Portia: Thou therefore endure hardness, as a good soldier of Jesus Christ. No man that warreth entangleth himself with the affairs of *this* life; that he may please him who hath chosen him to be a soldier. II Timothy 2:3-4

Day 18:
June 16, 2012, 7:50 a.m.

Sh'Rhonda Sawyer: *Let* love be without dissimulation. Abhor that which is evil; cleave to that which is good. *Be* kindly affectioned one to another with brotherly love; in honour preferring one another; Not slothful in business; fervent in spirit; serving the Lord; Rejoicing in hope; patient in tribulation; continuing instant in prayer; Distributing to the necessity of saints; given to hospitality. Bless them which persecute you: bless, and curse not. Rejoice with them that do rejoice, and weep with them that weep. *Be* of the same mind one toward another. Mind not high things, but condescend to men of low estate. Be not wise in your own conceits. Recompense to no man evil for evil. Provide things honest in the sight of all men. Romans 12:9-17

Connie, III: Stay alert! Watch out for your great enemy, the devil. He prowls around like a roaring lion, looking for someone to devour. Stand firm against him, and be strong in your faith. Remember that your family of believers all over the world is going through the same kind of suffering you are. I Peter 5:8-9 (NLT)

Joshua: Wherefore I put thee in remembrance that thou stir up the gift of God, which is in thee by the putting on of my hands. For God hath not given us the spirit of fear; but of power, and of love, and of a sound mind. II Timothy 1:6-7

Alicia: For God so loved the world, that he gave his only begotten Son, that whosoever believeth in him should not perish, but have everlasting life. John 3:16

Kellie: Hast thou not known? hast thou not heard, *that* the everlasting God, the LORD, the Creator of the ends of the earth, fainteth not, neither is weary? *there* is no searching of his understanding. He giveth power to the faint; and to *them that have* no might he increaseth strength. Isaiah 40:28-29

Kellie: Even the youths shall faint and be weary, and the young men shall utterly fall: But they that wait upon the LORD shall renew *their* strength; they shall mount up with wings as eagles; they shall run, and not be *weary; and* they shall walk, and not faint. Isaiah 40:30-31

Anthony: Lord, how are they increased that trouble me! Many *are* they that rise up against me. Many *there be* which say of my soul, *There is* no help for him in God. Selah. But thou, O LORD, *art* a shield for me; my glory, and the lifter up of mine head. Psalm 3:1-3

Crystal: Whereby are given unto us exceeding great and precious promises: that by these ye might be partakers of the divine nature, having escaped the corruption that is in the world through lust. II Peter 1:4

Portia: Pride *goeth* before destruction, and an haughty spirit before a fall. Better *it is to be* of an humble spirit with the lowly, than to divide the spoil with the proud. He that handleth a matter wisely shall find good: and whoso trusteth in the LORD, happy *is* he. Proverbs 16:18-20

Bonney: To the Lord our God *belong* mercies and forgivenesses, though we have rebelled against him; Daniel 9:9

Bonney: Be it known unto you therefore, men *and* brethren, that through this man is preached unto you the forgiveness of sins: Acts 13:38

Connie, Jr.: O give thanks unto the LORD, for *he* is good: for his mercy *endureth* for ever. Then they cried unto the LORD in their trouble, *and* he delivered them out of their distresses. Oh, that *men* would praise the Lord *for* his goodness, and *for* his wonderful works to the children of men! Psalm 107:1, 6, 8

Raymond: Have not I commanded thee? Be strong and of a good courage; be not afraid, neither be thou dismayed: for the LORD thy God *is* with thee whithersoever thou goest. Joshua 1:9

Day 19:
June 17, 2012, 7:06 a.m.

Connie, III: Children born to a young man are like arrows in a warrior's hands. How joyful is the man whose quiver is full of them! He will not be put to shame when he confronts his accusers at the city gates. Psalm 127:4-5 (NLT)

Alicia: Jesus answered, Verily, verily, I say unto thee, Except a man be born of water and *of* the Spirit, he cannot enter into the kingdom of God. That which is born of the flesh is flesh; and that which is born of the Spirit is spirit. John 3:5-6

Anthony: Be sober, be vigilant; because your adversary the devil, as a roaring lion, walketh about, seeking whom he may devour: Whom resist steadfast in the faith, knowing that the same afflictions are accomplished in your brethren that are in the world. I Peter 5:8-9

Kellie: Blessed are ye, when *men* shall revile you, and persecute *you*, and shall say all manner of evil against you falsely, for my sake. Rejoice, and be exceeding glad: for great *is* your reward in heaven: for so persecuted they the prophets which were before you. Matthew 5:11-12

bndsawyer: Thou shalt not take the name of the LORD thy God in vain: for the LORD will not hold *him* guiltless that taketh his name in vain. Deuteronomy 5:11

Connie, Jr.: Be careful for nothing; but in every thing by prayer and supplication with thanksgiving let your requests be made known unto God. And the peace of God, which passeth all understanding, shall keep your hearts and minds through Christ Jesus. Finally, brethren, whatsoever things are true, whatsoever things *are* honest, whatsoever things *are* just, whatsoever things *are* pure, whatsoever things *are* lovely, whatsoever things *are* of good report; if *there be* any virtue, and if *there be* any praise, think on these things. Philippians 4:6-8

bndsawyer: As for me, I will call upon God; and the Lord shall save me. Evening, and morning, and at noon, will I pray, and cry aloud: and he shall hear my voice. Psalm 55:16-17

Sh'Rhonda Sawyer: Charity suffereth long, *and* is kind; charity envieth not; charity vaunteth not itself, is not puffed up, Doth not behave itself unseemly, seeketh not her own, is not easily provoked, thinketh no evil; Rejoiceth not in iniquity, but rejoiceth in the truth; Beareth all things, believeth all things, hopeth all things, endureth all things. Charity never faileth: but whether *there be* prophecies, they shall fail; whether *there be* tongues, they shall cease; whether *there be* knowledge, it shall vanish away. I Corinthians 13:4-8

Joshua: Neither shall thy name any more be called Abram, but thy name shall be Abraham; for a father of many nations have I made thee. And I will make thee exceeding fruitful, and I will make nations of thee, and kings shall come out of thee. Genesis 17:5-6

Portia: I will praise thee; for I am fearfully *and* wonderfully made: marvellous *are* thy works; and *that* my soul knoweth right well. Psalm 139:14

Crystal: Unto thee, O God, do we give thanks, *unto thee* do we give thanks: for *that* thy name is near thy wondrous works declare. Psalms 75:1

Raymond: If the Son therefore shall make you free, ye shall be free indeed. John 8:36

Day 20:
June 18, 2012, 4:58 a.m.

Kellie: Let brotherly love continue. Be not forgetful to entertain strangers: for thereby some have entertained angels unawares. Hebrews 13:1-2

Sh'Rhonda Sawyer: Dearly beloved, avenge not yourselves, but *rather* give place unto wrath: for it is written, VENGEANCE IS MINE; I WILL REPAY, saith the Lord. Therefore IF THINE ENEMY HUNGER, FEED HIM; IF HE THIRST, GIVE HIM DRINK: FOR IN SO DOING THOU SHALT HEAP COALS

OF FIRE ON HIS HEAD. Be not overcome of evil, but overcome evil with good. Romans 12:19-21

Connie, Jr.: For I know the thoughts that I think toward you, saith the LORD, thoughts of peace, and not of evil, to give you an expected end. Then shall ye call upon me, and ye shall go and pray unto me, and I will hearken unto you. And ye shall seek me, and find *me*, when ye shall search for me with all your heart. Jeremiah 29:11-13

Raymond: But let all those that put their trust in thee rejoice: let them ever shout for joy, because thou defendest them: let them also that love thy name be joyful in thee. For thou, LORD, wilt bless the righteous; with favour wilt thou compass him as *with* a shield. Psalm 5:11-12

Bonney: I will love thee, O LORD, my strength. Psalm 18:1

Anthony: The earth *is* the LORD'S, and the fullness thereof; the world, and they that dwell therein. For he hath founded it upon the seas, and established it upon the floods. Who shall ascend into the hill of the LORD? or who shall stand in his holy place? He that hath clean hands, and a pure heart; who hath not lifted up his soul unto vanity, nor sworn deceitfully. Psalm 24:1-4

Connie, III: Live wisely among those who are not believers, and make the most of every opportunity. Let your conversation be gracious and attractive so that you will have the right response for everyone. Colossians 4:5-6 (NLT)

Crystal: Ye are of God, little children, and have overcome them: because greater is he that is in you, than he that is in the world. I John 4:4

Alicia: I will stand upon my watch, and set me upon the tower, and will watch to see what he will say unto me, and what I shall answer when I am reproved. And the LORD answered me, and said, Write the vision, and make *it* plain upon tables, that he may run that readeth it. For the vision *is* yet for an appointed time, but at the end it shall speak, and not lie: though it tarry, wait for it; because it will surely come, it will not tarry. Habakkuk 2:1-3

Joshua: God *is* not a man, that he should lie; neither the son of man, that he should repent: hath he said, and shall he not do *it*? or hath he spoken, and shall he not make it good? Numbers 23:19

Q: Now faith is the substance of things hoped for, the evidence of things not seen. Hebrews 11:1

bndsawyer: Beloved, if God so loved us, we ought also to love one another. I John 4:11

Day 21
June 19, 2012, 5:33 a.m.

Sh'Rhonda Sawyer: Finally, my brethren, be strong in the Lord, and in the power of his might. Put on the whole armour of God, that ye may be able to stand against the wiles of the devil. For we wrestle not against flesh and blood, but against principalities, against powers, against the rulers of the darkness of this world, against spiritual wickedness in high *places*. Wherefore take unto you the whole armour of God, that ye may be able to withstand in the evil day, and having done all, to stand. Ephesians 6:10-13

Connie, III: Go out and stand before me on the mountain, the Lord told him. And as Elijah stood there, the Lord passed by, and a mighty windstorm hit the mountain. It was such a terrible blast that the rocks were torn loose, but the Lord was not in the wind. After the wind there was an earthquake, but the Lord was not in the earthquake. And after the earthquake there was a fire, but the Lord was not in the fire. And after the fire there was the sound of a gentle whisper. I Kings 19:11-12 (NLT)

Kellie: Fear thou not; for I *am* with thee: be not dismayed; for I *am* thy God: I will strengthen thee; yea, I will help thee; yea, I will uphold thee with the right hand of my righteousness. Isaiah 41:10

Alicia: Thus saith the Lord of hosts; Consider your ways. Go up to the mountain, and bring wood, and build the house; and I will take pleasure in it, and I will be glorified, saith the Lord. Ye looked for much, and, lo, *it came* to little; and when ye brought *it* home, I did blow upon it. Why? saith the Lord of hosts. Because of mine house that *is* waste, and ye run every man unto his own house. Haggai 1:7-9

Raymond: The Lord hath heard my supplication; the Lord will receive my prayer. Psalm 6:9

bndsawyer: Rejoice in the Lord alway: *and* again I say, Rejoice. Philippians 4:4

bndsawyer: I want to give my praise report . . . God did it! Because of the power of the word I made it through this storm. If God brought me through this, I know He is able to bring me through whatever else is ahead. Thank you Lord. Thank you CC. Thank you (you know who you are) for helping me out in my time of need. Thank you for all the verses that have been shared. (I know that not all the verses are in for today.) I wonder how I made it before we did this.

Anthony: And when the day of Pentecost was fully come, they were all with one accord in one place. And suddenly there came a sound from heaven as of a rushing mighty wind, and it filled all the house where they were sitting. Acts 2:1-2

Connie, Jr.: If it be *so*, our God whom we serve is able to deliver us from the burning fiery furnace, and he will deliver *us* out of thine hand, O king. But if not, be it known unto thee, O king, that we will not serve thy gods, nor worship the golden image which thou hast set up. Daniel 3:17-18

Anthony: And there appeared unto them cloven tongues like as of fire, and it sat upon each of them. And they were all filled with the Holy Ghost, and began to speak with other tongues, as the Spirit gave them utterance. Acts 2:3-4

Connie, Jr.: Then Nebuchadnezzar the king was astonished, and rose up in haste, *and* spake, and said unto his counsellors, Did not we cast three men bound into the midst of the fire? They answered and said unto the king, True, O king. He answered and said, Lo, I see four men loose, walking in the midst of the fire, and they have no hurt; and the form of the fourth is like the Son of God. Daniel 3:24-25

Q: ...God is Love. I John 4:8b

Crystal: Seek ye the LORD while he may be found, call ye upon him while he is near: Isaiah 55:6

Bonney: Keep thy tongue from evil, and thy lips from speaking guile. Psalm 34:13

Printed in the United States
By Bookmasters